THIS LUMINOUS

PANHANDLER
BOOKS
UNIVERSITY OF WEST FLORIDA | PANHANDLERMAGAZINE.COM

Allan Peterson

THIS LUMINOUS
New and Selected Poems

Panhandler Books · *Pensacola, Florida*

24 23 22 21 20 19   6 5 4 3 2 1

Library of Congress Control Number: 2018956357

ISBN 978-0-9916404-4-7

Panhandler Books

Department of English and World Languages

Building 50

University of West Florida

11000 University Parkway

Pensacola, FL 32514

http://www.panhandlermagazine.com

University of
West Florida

For Frances, the luminous presence in these poems
from the beginning; for Lew, Kate, Carl, and Michael

Contents

from *Other Than They Seem* (2016)

from *Precarious* (2014)

from *Fragile Acts* (2012)

from *As Much As* (2011)

Introduction

Stephanie Burt

NEW POETS are commonly introduced as fresh combinations of familiar virtues, or else as ways to be au courant: the start of a battle, the crest of a wave. Allan Peterson's poetry—though it folds into its capacities such contemporary concerns as climate change, household divisions of labor, path-dependence, and mass extinction—is none of those things. Instead, it's something even more welcome: a trustworthy voice that sounds—in ways not tied to headlines—authentically new. You can hear in it, once you've spent time with it, and you can learn from it, a happier, more tolerant, more careful, and above all more attentive way to live from minute to minute, from year to year, in our shared world.

I'll take his most quietly joyful accomplishment first. More than any other poet alive, Peterson manages an intellectually complicated, consistently attractive version of simple appreciation, a sentiment that follows, for him, from the simple truth that we have just one Earth: "no hidden sun behind the one we have. No other world adrift / in the hall mirror." The poet grew up in Minnesota, went to school in Rhode Island, Illinois, and California, and then taught painting, and chaired an art department, for decades on Florida's Gulf Coast: most of these places, and some of the habits of seeing that painters must learn, can be seen in his verse, once you look for them. But reader who knew none of those facts from this life might be able to guess some of them from the poems they read like the work of someone who has to be either a visual artist or an observational scientist, someone who thinks about the way that what we see depends on what else we see, and about how to find beauty in so much of it.

William Blake saw the rise of the natural sciences, with their dependence on precedent and mathematics, as the enemy of intuition and wonder. For Peterson, on the other hand, they are allies; almost any page of Peterson's work can show the skeptic how science and awe, reason and illumination, reinforce one another: "Even the breath / has a butterfly in it and oxygen in foam as the air and water / brush past each other." "Even explanation can't shortcut mystery." Spend enough time in an art gallery and you'll walk outside feeling as if you still see things through picture frames; spend enough time with Peterson and you'll see real things and people, after you put the book down, in his own self-scrutinizing, thread-gathering, corner-turning, fine-tuned ways. Can you, too, envision "a sparrow's brown eyes, / the globe of an orange remembered from its peels"?

His poetry really does what the Russian Formalists of the early twentieth century wrongly claimed that poetry, in general, must do: it defamiliarizes the everyday, shines the dust off ordinary actions and objects, and makes all things it touches seem new. "EXTRA EXTRA" concludes "Local News": "a boy has left his room through the map on the wall." That's a child taking a nap.

It would be foolish to read Peterson's poetry and ignore his astonishment at the uncanny, the extraordinary, and the always-all-new nature of what we can see. And yet, it would be absurd, Pollyannaish even, to zip through without attending to its jeremiads, its protests against what our species has been doing to most of the other species on Earth. "So many so afraid of nature they send trucks to end it," he remarks; "If they looked back they might see their own long reluctant shadows / as if dragging their deaths behind." Having lived so long in Pensacola, Peterson knows that "the edge of a continent is a fickle thing." What looks firm, what has lasted for millennia, may crumble as fast as a thought: "this is all borrowed time but from what." Especially in his more recent poems, Peterson's environmental bitterness breaks through the mild observational shell. In "Trial," where we ourselves are in the "dock," the poet envisions two Keatsian allegorical figures—"causality going one way, morality the other"—watching our collective choices and, "hiding their eyes."

The dominant chords, though, are ones of appreciation. When human civilization is gone—or when everything but rats and roaches and pigeons and so-called civilization is gone—this poet would help us remember "that there was life underground and songs in the air/ before radio." He is one of those for whom beauty really is (in Emerson's words) its own excuse for being, one who hopes "that decoration would be seen for what it was/ integral and urgent and be given another name . . . longing." I have just now been quoting "Wishing," one of the Peterson poems I most wish I had written. The poem defends, as Peterson's earlier poem "Ornate" defends, poetry itself as ornament, as emotional surplus, as more than what we need for bare subsistence in adult life. "Ornate is being disparaged again but not by me . . . Austerity is something history does."

Poetry is what we do to fight back. We do so, not on behalf of any higher power, but for one another, for our shared and intimate future, for ourselves. "For the atheist heaven is the earth." Peterson takes his lack of belief in God as seriously as religious poets take belief, and he devotes himself quite as passionately as, say, Gerard Manley Hopkins to seeing and recording what Hopkins would call the creation. With "no gods needed, / no explanations," Peterson asks not why but how, and what, and where: "How does the dateline work How far west of recovery / does the arbitrary start How thin the appearances we trust." "There was no divinity in us or anywhere," he states flatly (sounding very much like A. R. Ammons), "only the exfoliating process of which we are a part."

And yet Peterson is a poet of reverence. Once he knows that we know they are only metaphors, he can personify wonders as "small gods"; in one of his garden-sidewalk-front yard scenes, "even the small gods get a chance, / and when I found one I called to Frances in sequins, / well rain drops, to watch the cicada." Such work recalls W. S. Merwin's reverence for nonhuman nature, though without Merwin's persistent wish that *homo faber*, and perhaps *Homo sapiens*, had never been. Instead, Peterson can admire what people do, either in "the intriguing comfort of an imagined past" or else right here, right now: "Look at the inquisitive miles fingers have put on pianos, / knocking softly though nothing opened." The seriocomic standout poem "Reminders"—a good introduction to Peterson's humor—begins, "Who speaks for the body? We do," then detours through Renaissance Florence before concluding with kids in skeleton costumes: fellow masqueraders, participants in human artifice.

Though it is dangerous to ask poets to inculcate virtues, Peterson's work can help us learn a few; in particular, his lines exemplify patience in their rhythms (they amble, they pause, they pivot, they never rush) and encouragement to see what he sees—"so open to everything"—creating a willingness to revisit his first hypotheses. The way of reading that Peterson's lines encourage also models, or stands for, the patience required to understand scientific processes, which require us to think about scales faster and slower than human time: "palm trees are fireworks but so slow we take them for botany." Because Peterson's attitude is so thoroughly monist, materialist, and nominalist—we are all made of atoms and electricity, and the same skein of words can potentially hold everything—he also sees all things as connected, even as cognitively adjacent. "An axiom / might be married to a stove, pitchfork to pine sap," "the wormhole near the sill / emerge near Aldebaran in Taurus" ("wormhole" is a pun: at once a gap in plaster and a relativistic passageway through deep space).

Yet it would sell him short, by a lot, to advertise him simply as a poet of science, of atheism, of ecological anxiety, or else of beauty found in things seen. There are people in his poems too: there he is, and there are the people he cares about, sometimes, as well. What he can do for things seen—for leaf-edges and lights—he can do for emotions, showing us how odd they are, and how they work slowly, beautifully, or counterintuitively. If you have an anxiety disorder, if you feel guilty all the time, you may recognize this not-so-hypothetical: "Let's say we made up stories from profound misunderstanding, / one of which was the necessity of guilt, a product like a dress shoe / you would grow into though it blistered and never fit."

To read Peterson is not just to notice detail, but to see *how it feels* to notice so much detail, to see, for example, how "each paddle leaves an aster in the river," and then to realize that, no matter what you see, there will be another bend in the river, another chance to reflect, more sights, and yet more. That kind of noticing, in turn, produces a kind of cognitive humility and a flavor of introspection, a way to remember that more data might prove you wrong: "whatever we suggest, there is always something / behind it, or beside it, or many at the same time."

Peterson's most important emotions, the ones his poems highlight, include quiet affection, curiosity, loyalty, persistence, restrained regret. The emotions are not so much what I expect from most contemporary poet as they are what

I would want in an ally, a co-worker, perhaps a spouse, surely a friend. It's easy to get passionate about mortal peril, or super-great sex, or lightning. Here is a poet who can take delight, instead, in "the way confident water softens red beans overnight." Peterson's self-complicating, self-winding sentences (and, one might assume, his partner and his marriage) also make him a gifted poet of marital love, recognizing what you get, as well as what you lose, from staying with the same person year after year. Even with "the whole thing slowing / so we have time to tell nervous stories / at night when the hot logs talk among themselves," still "as much as I touch Frances / it is not enough."

Not all the feelings here come off so happy. Peterson also proposes a new, and plausible, moral for the story of Abraham and Isaac on Mount Moriah: whoever you are, you should know that "you are capable of holding the knife yourself." He also depicts the familiar feeling (it is, at least, familiar to me) that your intense interest in minutiae, your fannish or collectorish obsessions, will repel your companions. One longish poem lists twenty of Peterson's favorite words, from "involute" to "equitant," then adds, "By this time none of my friends will be listening." At least, at worst, he can overhear himself: such a poet may get lonely, but he will never be bored. Even when exiled to the corner of a dusty classroom in childhood—so we learn in the standout poem "Private Lives"—Peterson found a spiderweb, "an archaeology of layers, of painted molding," and could fascinate himself with "the soft echo if I talked, / if I said I am not bad if this is the world." He has been saying so in verse ever since.

It's obvious what Peterson does not do: he will not tell complete stories, he's never overtly hip, he says little (directly) about his generation, and he has had even less to do with the parts of American poetry that try to defeat the logic of prose. Instead (like Ammons, like Marianne Moore) he offers *thought:* there are more ideas at play in a couple of pages of Peterson than in a stack of poetry-and-poetics debuts by many would-be Continental philosophers. Many contemporary American poets, by design and with justification, do not make sense; Peterson, however reticulated and knotty his clauses are, always does make sense. One of the great pleasures to be found in re-reading him lies in finding out how. (You could say the same about much of the natural world, comprehensible only when you look at it closely, and with the right tools.)

You can find precedents for Peterson's attitudes in the earlier poems of scientifically minded poets (Ammons above all), but his procedures, half argument, half diary entry, remind me at least as often of our great notators, our great journal keepers, in poetic prose: Hopkins, Thoreau, or the English poet R. F. Langley, perhaps Peterson's closest parallel among our contemporaries (and a poet that Peterson may well never have read). You might also think of John Clare, with his devotion to minutiae—for Peterson, as for Clare, "all flowers are / Forget Me Nots"—or of Thomas Traherne: "How like an angel came I down! / How bright are all things here!" Peterson, too, wants to cherish, to have cherished, everything, even the memory of lost teeth: "For this I sold parts of me under my pillow for a dime."

Because *This Luminous* gives us Peterson's work in reverse chronological order—the recent poems first—it lets us see where he is now before we can ask how he got there. The reverse chronology reveals more variety, but not much development: this poet, and painter, has been himself for a while (though who knows how he wrote in the 1970s; there are no dates on the poems, only on the collections, and the earlier comes from 1989). That said, what seem to be the earliest writings—especially those from *Anonymous Or* (2002), his first full-length collection—do more with people and dramatic situations and less with environmentalism and nonhuman scenes. Those poems tend to handle not fears about species extinctions but fears about individuals who might abandon us, or reject us, or die: they take place "in your chest where the hollow is," "where you can't look back, / where attraction shrinks stunned before care." If you want nuanced descriptions of shifting emotions but are not yet sure how you feel about mosses and ferns, you might try reading this volume back to front—you'll probably read it cover to cover anyway.

When I have written before about Peterson, I have tried to emphasize—as others have emphasized—his background in painting. If you are introducing him to, say, a critic who has not read his work before, his experience with brush and canvas and his long residence on the fertile, fragile Gulf Coast might be the first things you bring up. (His wife, Frances, and her background in environmental activism might come next.) All these are externalities, biographical facts, to be kicked aside once you have found your way into the poems. What you discover inside them is not a biography but a temperament, an orientation, a collection of special knowledge, and a way to make that knowledge (about plants, weather, marriage, domestic interiors, sadness, bones, amphibians, sea life, song birds, etc.) into so many extraordinarily patient, intelligent, sinuous or arboriform lines and sentences. Those sentences, in turn, produce entire pages that invite us in, that treat us well, that can teach us something if we are ready to learn, and that open up to us again and again when they are read and re-read.

THIS LUMINOUS

Turn off the light
The hemming begins at once
You hear the engine of the sewing heart
stitching into sleep so you won't come loose
Out the window light is still moving
that sees through your bones
I hold a flashlight to the fire in my hands
How can I see into my skin's little blue rivers
and not out from my eyelids
How can the water that holds up everything
slip through my fingers
How can we be this luminous
and people go right on talking

NEW POEMS (2013–2017)

OPTIMISM

The gift of the future was finding out
how wrong we were about the past
We were so open to everything
it was like unprotected X
We wrote words like leaves that fell
and turned in the current
as a rotating wing reducing pressure
on its cambered face produces lift

WORTH

How alive was the air and bare places dressed with webs

weeds from my childhood showed me the rich hours

jeweled insects July that liquified against my fingers

and meadowlarks spoke for the grass   I heard one today

For this I sold parts of me under my pillow for a dime

VIGNETTE

There is a heartbreaking earnestness to life

On the midway a man was selling chameleons

He had many on strings pinned to his vest

It was Royal Stewart plaid   They were trying

APPARENTLY

There is no *super*natural just the apparently

unlikely as cartographers that must have been afloat

to have seen cities and hemispheres from such altitudes

the way ants know to travel through drywall to the cake

BOTANY

I started a garden just flowers and watched
the cotyledons turn recognizable coming up
like pictures on the box warning of glycosides
in ranunculus water crowfoot and lesser celandine
They were poison in the book but that was once
said about tomatoes so I ate a another nightshade
just to see

DIRECTIONS

Emily started with a last line and then wrote backwards
to discover how she might have gotten there
and Dan stopped what he was doing and began painting
like the Renaissance to see if a development was possible
that would not end in Abstraction

O THE HUMIDITY

The air is largely nitrogen and often a pulse is visible
It comes to the surface like a mammal for a glimpse and
    breath
I know you have felt it in blood and heat   Even the breath
has a butterfly in it and oxygen in foam as the air and water
brush past each other and some aroma brings back New
Jersey fueling or falling in succession and then hydrogen
But what do they take us for telling us lighter than air
like the Hindenburg Jesus it must have weighed a ton

OUTVOTED

Governments are systems in which no virtue is perfected
no innocence preserved   Once the Yanomamo met outsiders
they began planning their survival   This is inevitable
In every such discovery everyone will eventually have to dress
in their feathers and fly in a winged horse to the capitol to ask
for justice   The pleadings will demonstrate how the roots
of the manioc have been damaged the disappearance of animals
and the silting of streams was like blood withdrawing from the body
Those with no trees and not enough parking will find the metaphors quaint

CONFESSION

I read the chemistry so I think of my windows
as thick syrup
and I do see a whole world stuck to them
so I believe it
Somehow twenty pelicans just now escaped
with their shadows
but the oaks and palmettos are struggling
wildly to get loose
If they can't do it with a thousand hands
how could we with two
Our predicament had been holding two things
true at the same time
It was worse actually   We knew truth between them
and did nothing

OH

Oh we say it saying numbers   O for o for zero

The Maya invented the Oh   One nine four Oh

That was my year   The sky had broken into pieces

blackouts here and ack ack in Europe

They had some 800 glyphs   Every fifth was a tracer

I remember saving fats in Minneapolis for the war

SUMS

Within the wind are small channels
capillaries the birds ride   bank as blood
before the tricuspid
A storm is like a huge lung breathing
and arranging its force numbers
Sleep waits in a small bag counting on you
Memory a frayed cinch string floating behind
Everything is hyphens and equals:
The nines live in the waves offshore
Threes in the heavens
Fives in the last hand waving
Zero is the ghost

HOW IT WORKS

A book is saved memory
A tree is memory saved as a book of leaves
This is not news
The leaves say themselves again and again
The pages remember the tree
and the leaves that have fallen onto its own
We saved each of them
to make others out of paper and wire
With each one we said
I remember   There was the elm
the rope swing was in it and the yellow bird

WISHING

Wishing on candles then blowing them out
Shouldn't that have meant cancel
or was it smoke not light that carried wishes
to the gods of luck that lived near the ceiling
and would grant anything for cake

In wanting I was led to extravagance

My philatelist wished for the blue English kings
the Penny Black and Inverted Jenny
the distant and multicolored islands Seychelles

My botanist wished for ferns and horsetails
the lush coat of trees like the road from Reedsport
to I-5 along the Umpqua
that had my name sewn into its lining

My theologist wished everyone to realize
that *this* was the afterlife and begin therefore
to live as if it mattered
to recognize those professing a next one
were equally likely to believe a gold thread
ran straight from Aldebaran to a clutch of hens

I wished purpose would be self evident as the ivy
of the arteries that the man dowsing at a rest stop in Utah
would recognize death and water were allied
that there was life underground and songs in the air
before radio that decoration would be seen for what it was
integral and urgent and be given another name   longing

I took a deep breath

HANDMADE EXPERIENCE

I am reading small books
that can be opened with one hand
and held as if cecropias
wings spread wide as pages

Amy makes them

They confirm my wish to live fully
in the intensity of silence
and within the beautifully accurate
language of *Gray's Anatomy*

Earth is a ~~bookmark~~ birthmark

I hold a cobalt glazed bowl
full of *Babylonia spirata*
from the Indian Ocean
revolving wishes into fulfillment

A fog ~~bank~~ book moves downshore
cohesive   opaque   yet ghost made

a frenzy of cells   a magnificent glimpse
a sunset sewn in gold threads
and I am still in love   all flowers are
Forget Me Nots

To protect such preciousness
colophons once bristled with curses

EX LIBRIS

The book says let us begin with respiration
I might say heartbeat but nothing
has a single cause and anyway this is not causality
but the breath of words
like birds near me pure nervousness at that

The book says normal speech is not inspiration
meaning the incoming breath
but poetry is not normal speech but a wren
whose feathered throat fills
with the staccato flight of a skipper

The book says water cannot read it writes
charmingly starting with a stream
then with the same vowels presses harder
overcome with endless inspired oratory
consonants carving the epic slot canyons of Zion

The book said memory was delicate as inheritance
sometimes remembering catastrophe
a truck of bees overturned on the Interstate
smoke calmed them so they must be related
to the jealous gods pampered by sacrifice

The book showed me the hammer and the anvil
that explained the ringing in my ears
as an armorer forming decorative protection

or the metal of the train passengers look out of
to see the villagers feeding on their herds

The book said future was the timeless dream
as if history and the present were delivered
to a faucet whose belief in plenty was inexhaustible
as a poem is always now   a photo always then
the present as a cabbage white on lavender

The book said life is full as the senses allow
the same for springtails as for the unspoken
languages of bone restructuring memory
an awareness that we should attend to
as the Paiute said even rocks have a song in them

The book said print was a hedge against forgetting
so one could repeatedly look forward to yesterday
in the fabulous impossibilities made fact
the movement of oak roots under the house
the nurse hearing your heart through two shirts

The book said we spoke with egressive air
but it was also possible to speak
with an inner voice   no sculptor in the throat
shaping air but holding breath like an apple
in our mouths   this was reading

The book was made of windows on paper
lives within them while outside people
who dream for us carry their telescopes

into fields and parking lots   waking dreams
and the last dream with no remembering

The book said the universe doesn't add up
the missing invisibles outweigh the known
like writing our names on impermanence
the smoky understated poignancy of things
from M74 to a hand carving a neck scroll

The book said mates will be found in the wild
agitation of midges above the blackberry
that the boil of apparent chaos contains fulfillment
the future sharpened to a point of intersection
like a few words loved by another few words

The book contained the history of the uses of skin
as paper is a feeling thing and the hope of writing
is doing it well enough to be doors to the dark
behind them anxiety turned to a floral tincture
indelible as blood and urgent as breathing sleep

The book said unintended consequences
marked the limits of understanding
said   "none the less"   then "all the more"
confounded by what the gall fly had done
to the goldenrod *Rhopalomyia solidaginis*

The book said we began with a big bang
even without us how touchingly we claim
a history before we were even possible

but yes I remember the heat and the light
I remember even then believing none of it

The book mentioned Andromeda as *local*
as if we should be surprised but I was
already seeing Mars in the front yard
squeezed between two twigs and a moon
uneasily adrift in a glass of water

The book was a medicine for many
Dun Cow dipped in water for the herds
but symptoms were unable to fall silent
I wrote   *body of water   body of work*
I kissed it   it was not made better

The book said speed kills but really
it's the impact and we were looking away
breathing deeply the gas of gardenias
watching palm fronds grapple with the moon
trying to move faster than uncertainty

The book said nature was indifferent
but I know if you bring bread crusts
it will surge forward to your hand
seagulls pigeons some birds with colors
like rubbed raw with a sink brush

The book described an original meanwhile
during which the world was assembling itself
from hot darkness   dust adding hope to shadows

fiction inhabitable and poetry breast feathers
it was the book of what for and what before that

The book had a reference listing tides
pages like waves named and numbered
for depressions hurricanes scolding the coasts
We take home fragments and empty houses
that the ocean let go out of hopelessness

The book said behold the philodendron
lover of roots and water that freezes
before it hits bottom at Chaco and equations
worked out in brickwork where we walk
The given is a jurisdiction   All rise

The book was a legacy from low speed history
Romans finally putting spaces between their words
the Maya positing zero and quantities clarified
identifiable animals and loaves being delivered
sometimes never reaching the page in front of them

The book said history was heartbreaks
stretched flat to catch the wind
a cargo of sad chapters like a privateer
sending regrets across a bow like warnings
a main hauled tight like rejecting surrender

The book said precaution had its shadows
assumptions   failures   misguided insights
anxiety   even a grey bird eating red berries

could be threatened and yes there was death
it would have been dishonest not to mention it

The book said finding another world depends
on finding the edges of this one and whether
apparent edges are really folds like patterns
on fingers and convolutions and all the other
family ampersands of which we know nothing

In spite of itself the book admitted most things
are inadequately explained like the second hand
skulls of history the origin of river blind fevers
a list of suspicions from Anonymous to Zimbabwe
in spite of histories repeating the same mistakes

The book was almost human it had a spine
that would fray in time and collapse poignantly
an appendix useful but not necessary   a voice
affixed to its pages we hear deeply within ourselves
dreaming between title and the end

WHAT WAS SAVED

This is the old world   the round shouldered hills
the rocks chocolate
the mountain from three sides and the toy cars
on the tiny highway
like watching a circulation of the blood

From here there are no emergencies
only occasional brakes like crying
experience taking the shape of the mountain
and the chill of the long sea

What we have of history is what was saved
and what happened to survive
a crystal skull   a shroud   a few coins
simplifications in Latin
foreshortening of eyewitness accounts

I heard a car like a heart in arrhythmia
Some law was being broken
speed limit   noise   someone leaving the scene
of heartbreak and famous last words
Then the first cricket began timing anxiety
Then unison pulsed the gulch

TRANSLATION

On the shoulder of St Jerome a bird
speaks but cannot write
and afraid of the past tense speaks prophecy
The saint is the bird's way
of delivering messages but translation is difficult
god's voice or not
and we have our own intentions adding a flourish
a guess at a thrush word
What will it matter   It cannot read

KOI

Koi converse in slow circles
of what we have not seen
Mercy
and the dark bottom of the pond
The recirculating pump we call
karma
is only a sound and mysterious
as well being
A comforting surrounding
to lives of endless destinations

HIGH FIVE

Your beautiful diagrammed sentences
still have not described what you're after
a heart wanting out from the dark to see
magpies and apple snails   modifiers   clouds
holding ruin and angels each with a harp

lyre lyre

High five meant the hurricane
approaching Texas was a power convection
like verbs preceding and verbs following
At such a distance the forecast says
atmosphere is keeping to itself

Not true   I knew its name already

NOTHING PREDICTABLE

The edge of a continent is a fickle thing

lisping one day bellowing the next
water hardly moving then rollers from Samoa
like reading "The Timetables of History"
only to have it end the year before your birth
getting the news but getting it late and out of place
finding a Venus Comb Murex
from the Pacific on a Gulf beach and remembering

this is all borrowed time but from what

ALTITUDE

Distance is the first understanding

We had come out of water colors
waves with visible fish in them
and entered the rock solid uplands
of Bryce and Zion red as slaughter

Height fills up the idea of empty

We saw future through a bird's window
sun streaks stroking the earth
colors that could be my ambulance
fire pulling itself apart into small pieces
all silent till jays mobbed a raven

Undoing is non-negotiable

Things seemed to have color enough
for one day draining by nightfall
like diving to the end of light
below a reef or singing a fever down
then sinking slowly like abyssal snow

Vision contains judgments of touch

From the butte red cows were corpuscles
moving and pooling   tadpoles thick
in the Smith River frilling the margins
of the fabric of speeds and urgencies
with vistas bleeding from the rocks

Gravity has unexpected consequences

Fan wind lifted the unframed Amsterdam
that fell and cracked like a brass cartridge
hitting edge on the plasma colored tile
Mollusks smoothed over irritants with pearl
tuning the stringed instruments of memory

Records set above 1000 meters unrecognized

Winter is a deep breath outfoxing shadows
winds dispersing ghosts color comes later
in the blood spots of christmas and the blue
of less oxygen so climbers so runners
acclimatize the sky conniving with them

Weight classes go from fly to feather

I was lighter after the hawk left
With its presence added to gravity
I had been weighted to my spot
my heart like it was a fist with wings
trading height with invisible hungers

There are alternate clarities

From here simple recognitions continue
in Latin   Cumulus   Nimbus sheaves of light
in crystals each name layered recollections
Italy in wisps of cirrus white as cake mix
Bernini making gauze out of rocks

ALIKE

Time is misunderstood in its own time and later in due time

like the tide that one day took a loose skiff and left a shark

both floaters or the song that arrived tethered to a neck scroll

as if a rope had been tied to equivalence slowing things down

as finial is final is finale like   you know   analogous not homologous

THESE WERE THE DAYS

In the house the desk was a heart
It ran the bookshelves and typewriter
with the little blood and death ribbon
of the Smith-Corona
It began to write stories of what if
one could live a life over
avoid the black failures and the red
faced embarrassments
I would not try it   I might not find you

STARLINGS

Little pieces of night sky gathered in hundreds to roost

and loudly discuss how quantum their swirlings were

like cascades of selfless electrons in unscripted flux

I listened to them marvel at their stunts

REEF

I found a description of a reef as being
the calcareous skeletons of various coelenterates
You can't say that to just anybody
Corals with creatures over them like a parade
A woman stood in a clear raincoat with streamers
and a transparent umbrella   She was a jellyfish
a colony of see through urgencies in unison
trailing strips of bubble wrap and strings
Beauty is the recognition of what we will miss
She asked if I could see her brain a colander

BLOOD

Everything red has some of its properties
carnelian alizarin a lake like other lakes
translucent and fugitive
After muskets armorers made gates and hardware
Running for our lives became track & field
Civility among the warlike never caught on
as did bathing in flags and fabrications
ritually dipping an arrow to remind the shaft
of its purpose

FULL OF BEGINNINGS

I am full of beginnings, the best parts
since endings so often go awry.
This is philosophy, the thrill of starts
and where they go.
For instance as much as I touch Frances,
it is not enough. Like white mice
pressing their pleasure centers, I am writing
in the shadow of my hand
and the dream I keep beginning
has the fractals of snowflakes
catching on everything, the whole thing slowing
so we have time to tell nervous stories
at night when the hot logs talk among themselves.
Not once upon, but Monday, when sunlight
through water on Hydrilla is the Northern Lights
airing its curtains and everything beginning
hovers expectantly above.

PLEASURE CENTERS

I believe in slow down
I became convinced by languorous sex
and the ponderous slow motion bodies
of the enormous Arapaima the Pirarucu
taking four men straining to lift one

the deliberate filling in between minutes
since minutes had expanded seconds opened
to milliseconds   nano   till a whole valley fit
with its rivers and the flooded might walk
waist high   walking by smoothing   by caressing
water away with each hand   a well oiled
motion slowed like paramecia in glycerine

and by a sign for caution   for stopping
for thinking it over   a horse seemingly dead
against a fence as we passed on the Coast Starlight
drinking the lengthening fathoms of luxurious details
windows turning from dark into trees
and looking away from landscape out the window
to the silver white wall and there was the other world
of complementaries at the same speed
afterlife as afterimage viewed backwards as if a chair
could be tamed by a lion and turned gold as a consequence
or a highway disappear into a silver milk truck

a sign for leaping deer   stalled midair
for do not enter   no turn   around   one way
indicated with an uncompromising arrow
mechanical fan looking   then looking away

Once we floated for a week in the same place
a house the river rising slowly like a deep breath
We were held back while whole trees swam the Willamette

With adagios so adhesive   all of the music
would not exit the French Horns   held breaths
and water remained even after the B flat sonata

We lingered in that space   slow as a house   breaking loose
from its nailwork heading ponderously downstream to the falls

Nowhere does it say "in the beginning
was the picture"
but sometimes it was so seductive and compelling
it seemed like clues to beginnings
Lines I saw myself making with honed edges
were added as easily to paper
as princes in manuscripts with pointed shoes

purposeful lines meeting in meaning
like fall in Oregon with all seasons possible
in a single day   my pencil and my moon
sharpened at both ends

When the past was past we had history
silent as a wing's leading edge feathered
though it seemed no longer aware of itself

It was all past actually and smoothness spoke to it
being also more silvery and dignified that way
and gray would be grey for the same reason
and angel-like with a long trumpet such as they used
dressed for painting in their best draperies
And some things demonstrated historicity
Frances doing crunches on a flowered bedspread
three sets of ten   roses reclining then alert
systole diastole   rest and resurrection

The unbelievable was meant to comfort death
Acceptance was a wish like a farthingale was style

We were willing to believe in those leggings
those wimples and poulaines but angels were a problem
even in the beginning those long trumpets
assumed they knew how to work metal into sheets
and roll and flare one end into a lily
and braze and polish   that they had smelters and metallurgists
and someone doing laundry for those beings in sheets

Words cast no shadows   there was no end to anything

We did not make up this world
it was right there beyond our comprehension
and close as the toaster and the stove
We made up another one and believed
in its invisibles bird songs
translated into baby talk English
shop windows borrowing thin slices from passers by
adding them to shoes and musical instruments
in the parallel life of merchandise

In the unmeasurable dark there was time
to think of the appendix that vestigial string
how it might be possible to draw a whole heart
with one continuous line maybe in silver point
oxidized bone on the page like something hammered
smooth lake the wind peens then softens
If Hell had the bats why wouldn't they want out
at considerable speeds

There was no divinity in us or anywhere
only the exfoliating process of which we are a part

In another I would be my own
I would be self cleaning like the oven
like a straw   like slow flowing life
blood streaming thickly into a mosquito

It would center on the edge of disorder
where creativity was
and it was never enough to say never enough
not being made of simplicity ourselves
There was no plenty after all
but we saw reminders just before sleep

context created itself
from whatever happened to be there
words on a page   pages disappearing
moments   sometime hours of great certainty
finding the maker of stalked eggs on the door glass
watching snow geese bandage the moon

To the seven basic machines we added
the air conditioner and hand calculator
with these we thought a nation was possible
but nothing could be done about the sound
of the door opening a name called
into the frightening night as if a room
storing the familiar

We tried the lever   the inclined plane
the pulley   wheel and axle   the wedge
We were so hot and tired of waiting
all the birds had their beaks open

we had a hard time with emptiness
creating explanations to offset the vastness
of ignorance the pleasure of symmetry
in spite of clocks telling different times
in different rooms of the same house
and blank pages were left over
at the end of a book

Empty meant you take it from here

from *OTHER THAN THEY SEEM* (2016)

TASK

A tug is passing like a cake of lights
push boat plowing the whole night
otherwise there was nothing
to indicate it could be passed through at all
or be solid enough to hold up the house
me having my shoulder to the door
a task oblivious and difficult
my deltoid and dream-stained sheets exhausted

CATEGORY 2

The instructive part of weather was "feels like"
hence the primacy of sensation over thermostats
Now something alphabetical is up to "I"
whirling offshore hugely famous with itself
and there was temperature and time
dressed like Thursday in a loose grey suit
a natural mechanism where at intervals
a door opens and a small wet figure strikes a bell

ATMOSPHERE

When I saw the sunset all the blue
had drained out of Nevada
the slow tree with the thin years in it
an empress in vermillion chiffon
drifting down behind the Sierras
After an epiphany or scare
one feels histamine tingle skin
I remember beauty is self inflicted
On a gridded floor I watched a spider
choose a path that graphed optimism
A pale moon rose like a ghost of soap

LIMITATIONS

We can hardly accomplish anything
straight out even explanation can't shortcut mystery
and make the world simple as lies
after all we know about complexity
So we try it the hard way
theater and film   poetry and fresco
little glass rods that can be twisted into horses

AGING

is one thing we do without practice
Our breaths wing beats just to stay aloft
Little speedups convince me
there is a bird that visits my heart
with the same flutters others have described
But this is my heart my bird
I feel its wings when it practices
learning to fly to the willow with my hair

PROCESS OF CULTURE

A dustpan beginning as a hand
sweeping crumbs or one thing into another
becomes eventually a tooled silver flatness
with a handle in the shape of a bird's wing
brothered by a whisk
Culture is a distance between you
and your hot meat antecedents
A fork for eating instead of your fingers
A hand on a cat that left a mouse on your shoe

from *PRECARIOUS* (2014)

(1940)

Terrible things began with me
in the midst of radio and lightning
People said such things had been going on
for some time but I had no proof
O there were books and pictures
and children had been poisoned
by whistles made from the stems
of cow parsnip and there were sad songs
and the sound of bombing
but I thought that was because there was never
a time when we weren't dreaming
I remember it must have been windier then
Snow swirled around houses
under an apparent bowl of stars
There were paperweights everywhere

REMINDERS

Who speaks for the body? We do.
Every eminence named, each fossa,
eloquent structures of shining bones
as if standing undone on a hill above Urbino,
artists making bright lines in bright sun,
bright language as the bones resurface
after an interim of flesh. Ribs, phalanges,
wings of the sphenoid, shapes named
for what they resemble, scapula a spade.
And how we look lovingly seeing a body
that does not clatter apart, that articulates
without ligaments, that presents in October
poignant reminders begging at our doors.

ALL THIS INSTEAD

He wanted it special so he planned on releasing
a dozen white doves sent from Connecticut
after reading the passage from Psalms
and the words especially written by his cousin
the poet composed he said as if music itself.
And the rows of oak so the sound deflected
and combined above the audience in a way
fractal like the galaxy and the same was true
above the ushers wearing gloves with a button
at the place where the palmeris longus meets
and feathers into the flexor retinaculum.
All this instead of just stepping into the garden
as it was where one *Vanessa* might be nectaring a rose.

EASY BELIEVERS

Last night tried to accentuate the stars
by staying darker than usual
the dark of the body inside the body
onyx as Satan's crows
suggesting it had been touched in places
with a hot wire like a skin
that powders from that same experience
We are easy believers
and it takes only some voice of authority
to say inside the body
is none of our business if organs shift positions
at night and a cure is to drink
nettle from a church bell or that to survive curses
a mandrake must be uprooted
by a black dog on a rope then struck dead

KNOWLEDGE FIRST

We call it knowledge first to be nice, then superstition
if it's theirs, then demonic if it means contradiction.
Remember the Tree of it, how dangerous, how nothing
    stays
in its place once you know feathers drop symmetrically
so the skimmer doesn't fly in a circle. The very idea
of *its place* is the forcing of facts into a philosophy
someone is paying to maintain. The moment the sugar
crystals surrender to syrup out of sheer curiosity
they start to rebuild again drying to a small city on the knife.
Lilacs are massaged along the fence by windy hands.
You can see them give and moan from their fingers.
This is what they told us we'd die from, wasn't it
—love, teeth first in the pinnate leaves, then the hickory
chewing on its lip lies to us again.   How after dying it
    recants.

SECOND SIGHT

No soul. No gods. No hidden sun behind the one we have. No
    other world adrift
in the hall mirror. No money back on the death offer. She said
    sometimes a baby
is born with a caul.   A skin veil.   A sign of second sight. That the
    common is not
alike each time and is therefore misnamed. The exceptions are
    numinous.
A child special-delivered with an onionskin letter from the
    shivering molecules.
A deep see-through angel. Meaning things arrive without asking.
    You just guess
and suppose until something answers back unexpectedly and you
    tell a friend
excitedly how it had wings and appeared right in the middle of the
    shopping center
with gauze for clouds and its own photographer. Look at what we
    take for normal.
The desire is so deep to be and be assured we are something other
    than we are
as when palm trees are fireworks but so slow we take them for
    botany. She smiles.
Teeth behind her lips show light can originate from inside the body
    along with the Dark
Ages that happen every night. We can lie down anywhere. On the
    grass. The dock.

Over each other and look below us into the microscope. First there
is nothing

till we learn how. Then everything moves and jostles. We want to
tell someone

as if we were Cortez. Shout. Write home. Sing our way to the
unexplored interior.

Remember forever since we can't predict. Life is continuous from
atoms to email.

More at both ends. We lament our crude tools. Words. Fever. An
old Smith-Corona

with manual return. A machine forgotten like the old days when it
was common to write

heavens with a goose feather as someone in the pageant with fake
wings reminds us.

SECOND OPINION

Used or ignored the dictionary retains its power like the plastic skull
that glowed on my keychain at night powered by the diagrams
and paragraphs of everything from aleph, our grinning bones, to ship knots,
a lexicon of leaves: lanceolate, ovate, palmate, and explaining the difference
between some stone-colored dove at Wakulla and another pigeon drinking
through its nostrils in a continuous stream to the final zed for lightning.
I've added *Amphineura,* the knuckle chitons, by being there in the curative
nature-as-pages, added fern floors in Washington and clastic rocks,
Gunnison's green aspens holding the 45-degree sky weft with its migrating
   spiders,
added the moon that barked out two clouds over Lake Quinault like speech,
added the anthracite jetties well before sunrise to the Pacific at La Push
where the Quileute practiced their canoes for the race to Bella Bella,
a singer's arms beckoning in as the words *love's hard luck,* like the rivers
going out fully dressed, the radio, the air above it that uncurled
like the questions when I asked, like party favors unrolling till the surprising
feather at the end.

BEGINNING AGAIN

There is a door that closes April
and opens May
It is paper and its numbers remember nothing
after thirty-one

Things begin again the way I can enter one room
and forget another
like a past life where the water has boiled away

In fifteen eighty two ten days
were removed from the calendar causing riots
for wages and lost birthdays

and today the day shortened an hour
and I became president
once again of the room behind the door

The ghosts pass again before the porch
the cruelest door
The riots continue now but more faintly

AS FAR AS I KNOW

As far as I know is not that far
I step outside to visit my mosquitoes
A boat winch strains to be a voice
There is no memory without remorse
The slightest passing thought
says poignant on the way
and poignant has a voice like that
a cry a winch lifting daylight and daylight
dropped from a great height

THE INEVITABLE

To have that letter arrive
was like the mist that took a meadow
and revealed hundreds
of small webs once invisible
The inevitable often
stands by plainly but unnoticed
till it hands you a letter
that says death and you notice
the weed field had been
readying its many damp handkerchiefs
all along

CONTINENTAL

We were sinking

The windows were filling with cities

as if poured into glasses

No one was thinking of drowning

No one thinking air ship

but there we were submerging

A captain turned off the cabin lights

We folded our tables   heading down quietly

The moon holding its breath floated up

A SIMPLE THING

Sometimes they will come
as if just born from the dark
between the houses or out of the opposite
of dissolve under the apple
from fog that sleeps in the fields at night
I look up from this line and a doe
is standing before me an empty space
only two words ago
It is a simple thing to lose the universe
an eyelid will do

WHETHER NEITHER

Whether neither in the sentence
is singular or plural
Whether heartbreak in Alabama
is one or too many
as often as the moons of Jupiter
Whether grey as yesterday is Paine's
or charcoal or the rest of Isadore
now inland and dissipating
Whether ardor is an instant or a list
Whether breath is wasted
sober cold rich are idle
Whether knowing all along is all

MY OWN RECOGNIZANCE

Trees blown out of the yards leave only flowers
like bows from lost shoes and their ominous heel-holes

The moon and moon snails have traded places
Trucks are trying to harmonize on the last passable road

If I am called on to explain the recognition of being
ultimately alone I say it is like the building catching fire

You are trying to escape with the rest and your sleeve
is snatched by a doorknob   You are yanked backwards

How disturbing the breaks in expected regularity
picket gaps   pines torqued to splinters   the mystery

of who lets off steam in a whistle that carries a mile
the repeatable joy of a tree frog housed in a broom handle

or taking a clock apart and staring at the impossibility
of reassembly   or trying to recreate a chair

with meteors in its wood and amber needles like a school
of minnows   First things first but easier said than sorted

First the blisters then leather relaxes forgetting it was skin
And longitude and lassitude how do they survive

How does the dateline work   How far west of recovery
does the arbitrary start   How thin the appearances we trust

We think we can stand in the present and reconstruct the
    past
from leftovers but look what is happening to Phoenix

on weather radar how braid and ribbon come together
like bees and wind at the entrance of a flower

I have been pleased to discover the concept of nothing
is only predicted by the body of the universe but not
    required

More likely is abundance   More to the point is the
    mythical
the little left to explain embodied in the common no less

than in the burning of elements in the interior of stars
and the certainty of thrill when Frances whose real name

I have yet to learn comes out of the bedroom wearing
only the silver necklace from Afghanistan

TRANSPLANTS

Whatever lives in a place already are the gods there: jaguars,
gulls, a water hummingbird as Mayans called the kingfisher,
right down to the chair upstairs at the Monet exhibition
for the King of France sewn in gold bees. Downstairs,
     Monet
has suggested another bed of iris near the pond, *fleur de lis,*
and Frances herself a corolla from a white blanket wakes up
asking for water. Monet the gardener doesn't match this
even with his caretakers. The whole bedspread her hair
blooms out of is covered with stitched roses, neat as an acre
planted at Creighton nursery, so every moment around her
is in flower and looked on with pleasure.   Outside, the sun
has gardened between bricks a pale fungus that
     complements
the paint.   Some windows have sleepy eyes.   Some shades
are partially open, and the ones that are see plastic necklaces
hung in the trees from the old gods that swarmed in
     February
together with the year around warblers.

I KNOW ICE

From afar life is zigzagged like a stick in water
you must drink it to know
and what really happened as a child is like a moth trying
to call back the worm
but in the midnight minus luck it can happen
I remember once I fit in a single sink
water was hand-pumped into   A chick from Easter last
came up the woodpile to look in
What became of it other than this picture
an eager beak nodding in its walk I do not know
I know ice was delivered by a horse
and a man with a rubber apron
Before that I was one of the embryo photographs in LIFE
a pink sloth backlit so my veins were the blood rivers
in an egg a delta in a lens
My hands began unfolding like a map on a napkin
isotherms   isostacies   America del Sur
There were War Bonds at the band shell at Lake Harriet
the woman I hoped for who was the name of the lake
Some of the last things I still believe years later
I did not fall in love   I walked   A mosquito ate out of my
    hand

NIGHT WISH

I want to leave the dream where I cannot decide in time
or worse   too late   that keeps happening
But it lingers   that dream   and the one before that
Where   flaming   I slave all night
instead of sleeping   or I am driving the paper car
and you are with me   and gravity
white lines combining and separating like the waves
that pass through each other
I love the world where tongue stands for a whole language
and tune up means tightening a wire
but I wish to linger in the dream that washed the moon
in the house that used feathers for bookmarks

PRECARIOUS

Winds and the half-winds and half that charted.
Heart and the half-hearted notched and noticed.
Still it's precarious to set out from Carthage
with just love and a lodestone, wet rope for ballast.
If the stutterer sings, it's smooth sailing.
If the whistler sits in the bowsprit, there's trouble.
The sentence will not complete, nor the voyage.
Always something more, another noun.
Now songbirds find the owl and scold the oaks.
Imagine the terror of jaws before the compass,
shoals as the premeditated curseworks of heaven.

ORNATE

Ornate is being disparaged again
but not by me
My mornings still have their flaming coats
buttoned with sunup
My trees are papered with gold leaf
edges making more moons in daylight
Austerity is something history does
in its guilt filled Calvinist phases
The crenelated fugues I wrote yesterday
with my pen of Venus Comb Murex
came elaborately into existence like woven brocades
satin anthologies spun out among the galaxies
experience sculpted to lace

EVERY DAY

Every day, if not sooner or more often
I find a small surprise.
Today a scorpion that overwintered in the latch
bird on the roof peak
like a prow and the house sailing faster therefore
to bring both of us and guano and oak leaves
closer to the coast where I am
turning the fish skull so the sun can bleach it
to go inside with the ormolu spoons
helmet shells and other treasures of the beauty
of death in life.

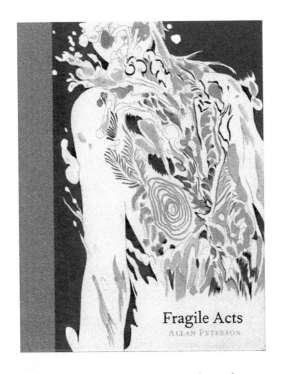

from *FRAGILE ACTS* (2012)

THE TOTALITY OF FACTS

The laughing gull that flew behind the fencepost
and never came out was the beginning
and then a hand smaller than my hand covered Wisconsin
with a gesture for explanation
In the afternoon there are pauses between the words
through which commas can grow like daisy fleabane
A fish with an osprey in its back emerges from the Sound
and nothing can be learned by more analysis
The book of her hair opens to its binding and I leaf through
the glorious pages of approval and that's not all
We could not have turned fast enough to catch
light and leftovers from so much of what happened:
the swift figures behind you like a planet's dark
companion   ships entering and leaving the hall closet
the real and imagined between which is no difference

HUNGER FOR SUBSTANCES

I know you have heard of them, the finches
adapted to diet
whose beaks accommodate to the shapes of hunger,
moon snails
which are said to be shark's eyes lost or cast off,
overgrown or cloudy
from disuse, while somewhere one-eyes cruise
above a reef.
And the paradox of the so-called living rock
out of which Petra
and Rushmore carved without a woman, amazing
but great waste.
And you have seen the young buy silver chains
against losing
a wallet but really are metals in place of plumage,
and a hunger
for substances strong as the moon that can't
take its eye off us.

MORE

We want more, but more is an emergent property.
It comes for you out of the same constituents
as when you were nothing but them yourself,
from the unspoken,   the far place
nickels disappeared with their buffalos.
Most of us never believed the ordinary
was that miraculous, the complex reducible
completely to a few brash headlines.
Look at the inquisitive miles fingers have put on pianos,
knocking softly though nothing opened.
Perhaps the pretty demons inside failed to hear
the twisting polonaise, hiding behind the curtains in
    brocade
covered with hunting scenes,
seeing the parade of notes festive though death-dressed.
One day you discover from the ads
suspicious has the same look as discriminating,
that greeny tigers have hidden their skins on the leaves
of *diffenbachia*, ideas like onions are dropping their pale
    slips
to the floor, that the garden is a smile around the house,
and around what is hidden by the house.

In the society of glass, one shatters from the least mistake.
Delicate is dangerous, the risks preceded by cautions.
In the fragile acts of memory even a goblet is poignant,
it shudders, it sings one wet finger on the rim.

In the silence of stone is the discernible eloquence of fire.
Redundance is characteristic of the ancient earth opening the
     hours,
geodes, little earths, riches instilled in the glassy magmas.

Transparent voices enter even the radios of Hotchkiss, Colorado.
Poignancy and singing load the air composed of nothing
but recollections floating above us into the atmosphere.

What was it like ask the songs, that world remembered
with all of history see-through and all of the present vitrines,
liquid life like rose windows, glinting with what ifs, as ifs,
precious, fragile, next to nothing.

It was like a laser pointed at a shattered vase in Corning
and having a portion of the fractured beam theoretically fall
on the faces of the apparently floating kings in Westminster.

Like Ruskin in Switzerland drawings in a few inches of
    charcoal
what he said was the edge of a mile of the Matterhorn.

It was like the geese on pink legs herded by Harry McCue
with the beam of a flashlight from pasture to the barn
while standing on his porch sheep-dogging their bodies.

It was like drawing at the same time water on the yard
as if Western New York had been cut loose from limestone.

It was a collection of collections, accrual,
like everywhichway signposts at crossroads.

It was how ribs for the barn roof were a boat overturned.
It was wearing expectations like a luminous string of perils.

It was more, it was greater than

>

It was like opening Webster's to "emptiness," void,
the invisible axis around which a rose opens,
the disappearance inside of the "o" of the ring binder,
a hole leading to nothing but another like itself
and a blank page awaiting explanation.

It was the heron that stood before me
like something from a manuscript, a guide,
and when it spoke the ancient opened, and I opened
another page to "adze," the instrument restoring speech
to the dead in the hands of Anubis.

>

It was like sometimes the overwhelming seemed enough,
singing when sung to, writing to when written,
coming early, staying late.

>

It was like the dogs were already howling,
the moon just happened to be there.

>

It was like all expectation, never starting from the dead
and working backwards to the passion of its advocates,
but starting from the baby, reliving the rest of us.

It was like we were trying to look famous once or twice.
forgetting that Pavlov learned to drool with his dogs.

It was a long way from equilibrium

>

KNOWING WHAT I KNOW NOW

That Ruth means compassion
and ruthless is without and brutal as we expected
That each form broadens
and explains the original idea which can take forever
That nothing is complete
till all examples have been outlined and demonstrated
every leaf in Umfolozi
That first Jupiter is smothered by daylight only
to be the first in plain sight
while Mars is in Destin, Florida, hidden behind the Tastee
    Freez
That nothing's in isolation
but is accompanied by lists of relations
That what will be called miraculous
is inevitable and dross-common
If I think I have exceeded my limits they were not
If I say the two magnolias
in the yard are like paired lungs from which singing
is breath from the leaves
I am nowhere near what the normal will allow

GREY AREAS

Things are getting fuzzy when you see the words
aeither, elan vital,   fixed stars.
or hear someone say that is absolutely impossible.
It got no better when Mrs. Witherow
put four oranges and a flashlight on her desk
to explain the equinoxes
and then said they were seedless.
The world was swirling.   How could that be so.
What about the miles of California,
what about the bees, the tiger perch
in Buck Lake spewing fry, what about the promise
I might see the light on the heavenly body
of someone I had not met yet.
What of the egg stories, anthers, pistils,
the sponge that was a plant, the plant that was an animal.
How much of this was lies just breaking us in
for the increasingly terrible to come.

FREQUENT FLYER

One does not tell the future   it tells us
when it gets here
People call and though I say wrong number
they call back
Last night I saw trampled grass where a deer
or refrigerator slept
and with light through lace like moon through leaves
during an eclipse
the whole room rested many times on your shoulder
It was like sitting on my leg
then rising up and feeling the stars pass through
each blood cell
You turned and glittered minutely like a mirror ball
like a lens to pleasure
But I have awakened after working all night somewhere else
just to take aspirin for sore shoulders
and thought maybe someone lives here with my name
or the lines in my hands are maps
to my aching other life folded in a fist
since even the moon sometimes keeps its one eye closed
above the whole population

LOCAL NEWS

In the old days news stayed nearby
           sometimes never leaving the scene of its origin
News that spread was meant to convince us for effect—
harrow making ribbons of the man in Kansas
           who blasphemed machinery
how lightning touched a silcock and soured cows

The local news is motionless and dries
around the event leaving a hardly perceptible ring
           Sometimes a marker will be placed near an incident
so readers must go to it
instead of leaving to wander the country mouth to mouth

Last night in the yard I passed Minneapolis
           but it was only gardenias calling bees
As a child I knew I was sleeping when I began
falling though still furled in my sheets
           and I would look over other people's shoulders
to see what they were reading
The headlines the footnotes
           EXTRA EXTRA
a boy has left his room through the map on the wall

There was an Era of Ashes
It has not passed
There was an Age of Labored Breathing
It has not passed
There were centuries of Paradisiacal Waters
They are over
There was a decade of wax hands
There was a season of Too-Tight Strings
a Spring of Sharp Edges
A week of Folding Birds out of Paper
a day of Coin Silver
an hour of Renaming Bones
There was Minute of Not Here Not Now

Wait a second . . .

We lived in these bodies from the beginning

even when daylight was getting up before we did
We lived together and apart and lived on salt water
on the short-grass plains, on nonstop talking

>

We would wake up talking of another life
Within writing the same would happen
our eyes would be open, staring how the trees
scuffled up a hawk from raw materials

Our question was always what did you dream
when I wasn't with you

The bodies had nonstop dreams in them

Pictures of the body were not the body
but with them we could find our way

In one illustration the palm of a hand opened
to catch broadcasts of song watercolored noises
laced with life directed to the ossicles of the inner ear

shading the eye cupping the auricle

listening as an illustration explained longing
how the earth was humming the sun vibrating
like a bell

>

The body was not a book though it had an appendix
and miracles and disasters a beginning and an end

>

The unknowns sang down the sun   arpeggio   arpeggio   rest

The sadder the bodies the harder they whispered as they
    passed

>

We saw crows in the zodiac, roosters told the wind
We saw a plaid blanket asleep in the dog bed, dog or not
We saw obligations, the number of things depending on us
including the overwhelming from which we were
    indistinguishable

>

We could use yesterday's clouds all over again
the old light and glass and reflections of the leafy yard

We would watch for the edges of outside becoming inside
and the sign at Mike's Garden saying the ladybugs were in

NEGOTIATING WITH DETAILS

I don't know anyone you know. I merely leaned over
the dock to handwash when the bottom up and shuddered.
A stingray large as a card table resting in my depth of field
floated off, its edges rippling, and I refocused to understand.
These things happen to remind us of the great community
where no one knows anyone. But through such revelations
is reunion, and implications of parallel things lost in hearing
despite the beautiful ampersands and treble clefs on either
     side
of our heads, the low hum of bacteria, flagellates dividing
like tape unsticking, imagining music is just background
till that one song and you drop everything to listen. The
     words,
partly obscured by a child's milk moustache, a blanket
     moving
back and forth over their sleeping bodies not by their doing.
Maybe you're just anxious. That x implied in the middle
of the words like *crossroads, crosshairs.* There there.
A *shhh* of assurance like the   x   spoken in the
     overwhelming
sound-scale vibration of ocean and Xochimilco

LONG DISTANCE

Astronauts say their dreams are like earth dreams
but the people are floating.
Last night when Frances answered her dream phone
I was down under the pastry layers
of sheets and blue throw. Later she asked did I hear it.
No, I had been orbiting myself,
misreading a box in Carol's kitchen "cloudless" for cordless.
At night when stars fall on Alabama,
water goes granular and steps back, dreams improve us
with their thick pastels, revisits in tints.
Maybe the astronauts called from their cloudless telephones
with news from Long Distance:
Romans invaded Arabia Felix, Columbus discovered Ohio.

There were echoes speaking to emptiness
There were voices saying something in Hawaiian
whose vowels washed over each other like water on new lava
there were handwritten letters of enormous power
There were names that floated like scarves above shrubbery
There were numismatists and philatelists
and multiple personalities of light
There were flags snapping like crisp footsteps
There were trees whose leaves were identical adjectives
There were certain words unavailable on Sundays
things so compelling illustration was unnecessary
There were serious times when appropriate dress was latex
gloves and paper shoes There were heartbeats like glass
There were stark reminders

Let's say it took acres to confirm the lights were moving
away from us, though one was Freeman's kitchen window
and the Red Shift, like the rate of inflammation, was Howard's
bloodshot eyes from another night of bourbon longing for his wife.

Let's say there was the world of mirrors that made things closer,
miles of fence and the four lights connecting pasture to the stars
and interstates, acres of miles of longing and remorse.

We could see how many potshots had missed the moon,
heard how many frogs made the sound of water for the lake

We saw the sign of cupped hands, the hearth stones,
the three-starred belt, the sword of Orion containing a galaxy.

>

Nothing explained the widening dark

>

Let's say the wet sky early was alizarin and loving
merely opening its echoing dark eyes, rivers,
rivers saying their secret non-consonantal names,
big long liquid ones that gargled, and equally
the rivulets echoed smaller from their cranny floods

Let's say we could not make maps fast enough.
The genders came and went. This for a minute,
that and back like the Mississippi that spills its banks
then retrieves them, all the big redfish, males.

>

Let's say we were blood cells in a larger being, or the planet was,
and we were the platelets and fractions.
Or we inhabited bubbles in a boil of all the brocade angels of the Orient,
while at night we heard insects open their packages,
a vast crackle unwrapping around us.

>

Let's say it might have been only a moment of high sodium
that separated songs on the radio from the whole house
as off in the distance cities could be seen swaying,

>

and it took only a slight constriction of iris to separate the gar
from leaf shadow at Clyde and Niki's paradise in paradise,
in the orchid and grass-dense glass-slick Everglades

Let's say it was like being in a maze of neurons like a brain
where nature was richly thinking to itself

>

Let's say we made up stories from profound misunderstanding,
one of which was the necessity of guilt, a product like a dress shoe
you would grow into though it blistered and never fit.
Its failure was supposed to be your fault and you paid with your life.

Still, don't think we hadn't noticed the wheels on the furniture
that could roll away at any moment as if a stage set,
how the carved chairs with wings and garlands were prepared
to fly off from the living room scattering flowers,

and what were their shapes anyway but straw fill and wires,
how could one wake up right in the middle of one's body
and be lost even when the bedclothes filled in
and furniture occupied again its convenient pretenses.

>

Let's say it might have been only humidity, the clouds
all racing and erasing, the shaky longhand of birds
coming and going, even the oceans never decided.

Let's say how often we woke just after daylight was opening
its complicated watch, the chickadees *tsk*ing
long minutes from the oaks, one dream having let go
at the last minute its daylight-saving heartbeats
on which the doctor eavesdropped with a rubber hose.

FAMOUS CANARIES

Once when half the San Carlos was demolished we saw things
sprayed on the walls about someone named Chico we never suspected.
Then Liz called. She'd met a Brazilian and her headaches went away.
Perhaps she was nervous after her father and then one brother with no
   warning
dropped like a stone leaving the shower and it was dangerous for her.
As if what happened underground was suddenly visible the dust was so
   thick
from destruction I thought of past miners and their waltzing mice
so active in their wire cages any slowdown was serious. As hard to think
a man might take an animal into the earth to be his next to last breath
as thinking she would leave for Arizona with another name as protection.
Her X husband still looks down on the bay and its regular breathing
the way she remembered twice a year goldfinches sulphured the air
to and from Manitoba. Glittered like dust. Or the soft and predictable
coal-colored fish crows that loaded and unloaded trees below their
   window.
Both directions have their risks. When they broke through to the miners
in Wheeling they'd left notes for their loved ones as the wall above
   Garden Street
made those boasts for someone as a predictor of some wild promise in
   the dark.
Now he is coming up for air. His legs are moving. Must be dreaming on
   his wheel.
She is closing her eyes in her yellow nightgown. Not a peep out of her.
Just retelling the simplest fact is drama. So far nothing has exploded.

NEEDLESS

Four birds carved in Thailand with skill that can miss a few feathers,
be painted differently each time, and still be truthful.
Imagination is creating the possible, its best work.
Gaudy-winged frogs, four-legged whistlebirds whose horns curve back
to be handles are strange only till they find one in Suriname
and feature its habits on Discovery.
That little stick-sound we know is bare feet in slippers,
that little blur of mouse scratching its cheek with a hind paw,
the wasp seeing pathways into the violet light, swatter arcing to the fly
feeling the railing with its mouth like a blind lover,
the yellow dots, black, magenta, cyan, hovering together like a vertigo.
But today a Spanish Dancer nudibranch and angels appeared in the
    newspaper,
thousands in plastic bags taken wholesale from rivers of the world.
Stop. There is no need to spread the animals everywhere.
No reason everyone should have a collection including a few of everything.
That is what the mind is for.

HITTING THE HOT SPOTS

Carol who would not hurt the fruit flies heat-stunned
on the red bedspread under her goose-neck reading lamp
slipped paper we still call typewriter under two and moved
them closer to the phone hoping they'd recover.
She imagined how things small as punkies or dixie midges are
picked up in storms or tornadoes and live a whole life moving
from the first fingering updraft in Texarkana through the dust
-fisted dynamo sidewinder ending the other side of the trailer
park in Mission Kansas—that standing in the stereo half-acre
of Vivaldi cranked to nine is a kind of pressured equivalent
to an afternoon alone in Denali's live silence or Biscayne afloat
above coral with a snorkel a larva turning slowly as one
of the Gulf Stream's glassy animals Jeffersonian and Emersonian
at once and closer to the sun. When she whirled and slapped
a mosquito and missed a red hand stayed on her leg throughout
most of the chapter on Self Reliance.

HERE AT THE INTERSECTION

A mute TV is just another window deprived of dialog
The figures seem curiously insane   A man speaks to graduation
from the stage with such electric distortion no one can understand
anything behind him still everyone proceeds as if nothing is wrong
They listen and line up for their incomprehensible diplomas
Between the blood meal and recognition are the sauces & forks
the left-handed napkin & the 3-spooned heraldry of metals
Culture is putting more equipment and ritual between us
and what we are actually doing By the time we are fully civilized
we will have obscured the origins of everything Here at the intersection
are small white crosses After the hurricane the scrawled names
of insurance companies appeared on the leftover walls Scrolled names
The figures seem curiously insane You cannot see a thing long enough
to understand   Mr Lincoln pulled back the curtains on the French doors
and left the White House on three occasions to have his son dug up
just to look again upon his face

from *AS MUCH AS* (2011)

AS MUCH AS

I have taken my chair into the undergrowth.
I sit above the dog long gone.
Around me an oval unfolds, the arcs of my vision
like the simplified maps
of the Middle Ages relying on Scripture,
not on looking for detail,
a world in a circle with no moving parts.
But this is not simple.
It would take days of naming to begin
to announce my visitors,
seeing within seeing like Hooke or Leeuwenhoek.
Said this way with exuberance,
it may fail to resemble any place you know.
But that is the way of attention,
it brings more than expected. And so before me
is the hot and moist, the four
elements and then some, the azalea as the answer
to iodine while spider silks tell the wind
better than the nylon sock or brass chicken on a rod.
And what looked alive was alive, and alive
within alive, and alive within that.
As far as I know. As I can see.
As far back as I remember. As much as I can stand.

HURRICANE IN HALVES

By the time half the hurricane had passed, nine candles
had pooled in their saucers,
the cypress split in two above the Toyota. Before they
   extinguished
I could barely read Robert Graves,
and in the diminishing flicker "groves" became "gloves"
and the Caslon wavered on the page.
So in my reading it appeared the sacred gloves had closed
   around oxygen,
had twisted the weather till the cypress split lengthwise.
In the other six hours the Romantic was carried upstairs
with the clothes and photos.
Birds blown from their nests were dizzy trying to recover,
our once local insects were entering Atlanta.
So maybe the Big Bang was believable after all, maybe an
   axiom
might be married to a stove, pitchfork to pine sap,
any stair might be cousin to a ladder and the wormhole near
   the sill
emerge near Aldebaran in Taurus.

SO TAKEN

The hours are so taken with themselves
planning what their gathered minutes will contain,
and the beach peas are so busy
portraying the ocean because they live by it
though their translation of swells into petals is imperfect
spending time to devise keeled flowers
as lifeboats to save themselves,
and the present is so beside itself, stuttering
into something almost tangible that takes up space
like writing a new love's name all over your notebooks—
the only instance of making a word more solid
by repeating when ordinarily it dissolves—
clinging expectantly to the surprising irregularities
as door glass holds houseflies.

THERE I GO AGAIN

Small birds are wisdom while the large are hunger.
No, that is another theory altogether.
No one could answer for all those restless apartments,
for the nests like axioms in the window angles
as if mathematics was certain as a sparrow's brown eyes,
the globe of an orange remembered from its peels.
Another is the reason the covers of my books curl volutes
like exquisite pleasures there on the deck rail courting sun,
or that tissue enflamed is first itself with no explanation
until something in the wild riot of the blood decides
on erection or fever. There I go again. I am like the ants
scrambling, unable to find the boot that ruined their
    nursery.
My guesswork is passing as purpose that satisfies worry.
Why the chickadees bathe in the drip plates.
Why a man must wear arrows while chained.

WRONG NUMBER

They are within hearing but unheard
even when you hold them to your ear
the way people will touch a photo
in a private ritual. We answer.
There is an absent voice in the middle of static.
There is news we are not getting
even from those who may think us a restaurant
but one number off. Or maybe they know
and it's just reservations. Someone hungry to talk.
If they might just lean out their voices
this could be the call they want after all.
It could be the unexpected answer
like the chair that lifts you up when you can't.
It could be what they need before dinner.
We might say appetizer. Might say news like a protein.
Might say everything that can be made
special in the dark with an egg and green leaves.

BAD NEWS FAST

Long stalks drowsy, short ones nervous.
We were agitated like someone mowed around us.
left us standing for some special attention
while the sky toppled over. And that's not all.
Its surprising weight had us worried.
Silver birds had stayed on their halves and quarters
unless thumbed invisibly for luck.
The mail planes stayed grounded on their stamps
while absinthe in the form of a lime-clouded storm
was headed down our throats and up
through the sandy shallows to the fogged-in moon.
That's when I heard the bad news fast that spread
accurate as bats led by their echoes. Even the flies
stopped rubbing their hands in satisfaction.

DISTRACTION

We want to read and sing at the same time
We want to say no place lacks bacteria and be sure
We can want to believe time
was altered by our presence that martinis
and opium harbor gods
We do not want to hear "returned to normal"
Normal contained us
We want that edge with an exit
We want to say rhyme or reason as if
that meant a consequence
connected with another world as fallback
We want to remember
in the beginning distances were so vast
nothing had voices but needed translation
and began poetry where we stepped in to listen
and notice repeatedly stars
were a belt and sword and contained a galaxy
We were just getting comfortable
when the signer misspelled sygyzy
but who could blame her
what with everyone staring at the stars
rubbing dangerously together on her dress

THE USES OF NATURE

It could have been dawn splintered by the sill
or some bright planks of yesterday
painted but forgotten and leaned against the wall
But I do not pretend an afterlife
not even for qualities   That is why it is so poignant
what you do with this one
Almost no one is born at home light or day
and no one is less mysterious
At the festival yesterday a woman sold beadwork
She made ticks and mice
and scorpions   a platypus   a flea
She said for a child the heart moves over
and you begin to think of mint and unusual animals
No one is making these rats
This one is nothing you would know of she says
like people in paintings
that pretend living pretend movement
Do you have the dog that eats the moon   a missile
No those are things men want
things brutal and useless   But we are the women
We string secrets

SOMETHING IMPORTANT

Whose heels light up with each step
from pressure of the *avenidas*
going one way, *calles* the other,
laces where they cross,
have steps like soft coughs coming
from next door.
It is to be expected that in explanations
speed will fit into the metaphors
along with footbones and names of shore birds
for what they do—turnstone, skimmer,
and the way I think of your body beside me
like a hurdler in love and lofting backwards
arching over a bar, things linking up
by themselves, a pattern sewing Paraguay to stars
enough to give you the idea
something important is happening and something
important could be said in something
fragile as a poem about the capability of blood
and running as the joggers are joined
by bicycles with little reflectors on the spokes
so the lighted heels and eccentric spinning
join the moving stars and the fixed stars,
some in Orion, some along the driveway.

NO GODS NEEDED

Saying bird is too big
    saying swallow is
Saying syrinx and all songs gathered in the throat
Saying those
who had globes were privileged those
on metal stands or those in the libraries
whose bearings were silent in their walnut carriages
    But I had a world map
that covered my wall above the painted radiator
Like a bird aloft I could see everything at once
    So no gods, no saints, just finches
No intercession, no afterlife,
    no souls smoking from the body,
no expectation but a dream
While I water
I see them visit the feeder So no gods needed,
    no explanations
It is enough to know they are finches,
and gold, and crave thistles

LYRIC

Something's got the Mergansers going:
       an opera   The chorus
diving and flapping like flightless maniacs
       Reminds me of a song:
If whiskey was a river and I was a diving duck
as if to say simplify   enjoy
throw up your hands to the waitress
       Dive Dive

A semaphore has three choices
       in infantile colors
Hold up the avenue is one   Green is vanish
like slugged shots
       Now the fishermen in slickers poling home
with the dead engine
pause to ask if I have an oar they could borrow
They move off singing caution
       pass the flask   It's dark at the bottom
and caked with weeds

MAKING SENSE

It was a song I loved but I skipped singing
and went down where beach peas wired up the pines
       and sharp-shins came for the catbirds.
New smilax had not yet hardened their horns
and were so many tomato worms.
Docks along the coast looked like a thumb piano.
       I listened.

We drink to the future. We eat to it. We have no choice
chained together by hunger and expectation.
       There on Solidago is a red admiral—*Vanessa*
whose worm I know and its host—nettles
and the grey fox stepping away from the buckeye
       lemons ecstatic with sour
two end days rafted to a week. There is no "making sense,"
       it is sense already.

AS IF GALVANIC

As soon as I sweep, the thrashers put the leaves back
where they prefer them,
millipedes scattered, earwigs
      applying their calipers to gravity.
I leave a minute and the red skink enters my chair,
      an articulated sunset drawn down from the trees.
I sit only to be an Indy of flies,
      a galaxy famous only to itself.

The minute depth was invented things began falling,
      blue light in the ocean,
the ideas of who we were, sky into the skin of book pages,
      whispers heavier than rain.
Around me the raw material, heat-induced, slippery,
      the mapping gnats, the dry and polished swallows
that cleave or shatter off like electrons.
      All this is drawn silently together,
though nothing like cellophane with its sounds
of electricity's sophisticated wrecks,
      nothing like magnets' spinning and clicking little dogs.

ONE OR MORE

Starting with greyblue-grey like East-Southeast,
>   moisture made Tuesday out of ants on my white chair,
sun behind a loon and five mergansers.
Last night I held a stem that grew in my hand by adding water.
I demonstrated waxwings for Frances,
how they flew close together, each finger one or more,
>   into the pear, into the pine tree,
running bowlines between, and Turk's heads
and double Matthew Walkers; how they flashed like olives.
Then the difficult began:
>   the material boathouse, the double birds with names
and shadows distilling forms, the two white boats like shaved clouds
that slowed and waved as *Betsy* passed *Distraction*.

WHIM OF THE MINUTE

They matter, but not for long.
Each second clicked to attention by a charged arrow
        pointing to doors that will not open though we wait.
The hour is philanthropic, the minute a miser,
concealing the otherwise least uppermost
erotic serenity of convinced societies
        caused merely to open their eyes momentarily.

Its very tail makes a river of the fox,
        raccoon a sleeping creek in the leafed trees, a trickle
in the worms of measured pleasure,
all eating their pasts.

Second is the whim of minute that exchanges space
for candles. S was mentioned as the living river,
C was death,
        body-curl of the life-threatening.
When duration was certain, each cabin was given a boat
        light blue to match the weather.
I cannot even remember were the flowers near the house
white or yellow in the afterlife,
        what crisp lilies traveled within minutes of the alphabet.

TOUCH AND GO

One gull touches down.
A moth takes its place, rising like a second thought.

Reality is both created and displayed.

Shore breaks, on breaking,
        become amphipods and crabs, scattering
to saw grass.
        Take and give
like the pass it on notes in school.

Little can resist this touch and go otherwise,
        this plenty for us.
But the gods have never been happy, always
coming to earth, butting in,
        to see if their pictures are still above the mantle,
their carvings stuck in the archways,
        if we saved their threatening letters,
their lies about life.

If all else fails, if the cameras
we designed to touch light into memory despite them
might prolong their descent,
        change them,
into answers without being asked.

THE SPEED OF LIGHT

Despite its reputation that nothing exceed it,
it lingers on the pond,
leaves only reluctantly from the nervous
silvery cottonwoods
gathered at the edge like a camping family.
But once vanished,
it stays out all night in another galaxy
leaving breadcrumbs to get back.
That's nothing.
I can be here one minute where the strings
of the driveway
are purposely united during daylight,
then to Jupiter and back
where one harebell starts the yard in its frenzy
of reexplaining.
What takes its place appears lovingly
like caressing a pet,
a Lab starting black and ending golden
as we float in our bodies
of blood and rubble so rich we'll hardly miss it,
a song at the end instead of a period

THE SMALL GODS

It is sometimes only a matter of mentioning the jewels,
the mockingbird's gold eye,   the toad's,
the skins beaded and gem-cut like goannas and pangolins,
and especially diamondbacks.
Isn't that what we're talking about, how the simplest glitters
like treasure, like a crown,
how the innocent holds a key to what we call paradise
which is not exotic, but so ordinary
we miss it encrusted on a leaf or stuck to the sidewalk.
Here even the small gods get a chance,
and when I found one I called to Frances in sequins,
well rain drops, to watch the cicada,
or she calls me to the owl in the red cedar, the two shoes
eyeing each other by the bed,
the weave glistening heavenly out of plain materials.

DEATH ABOUT LOVE

It is a style—the boots that demonstrate
how ankles collapse—
as now that of the orphans whose fingers barely reach
beyond their sweaters,
the patient's lost hair, fur, the backwards hat.
We have skin, so it is unnecessary
to wear that of another.
It would show we were lying about compassion, death,
about love, about the oils of anointing
delivered by a dove for Clovis of the Franks,
or an angel to the kings of England.
So they are messengers, and the knot above the foot
speaks to destiny and sprains,
travel with a body, the body that dries out
and crumples like a shoe.

NO URANIUM

As if time moved slower by the fire extinguisher
than by the phone
As if "right now" could be held in your hand
and examined
like the plain-faced decorations on a cup
spoken to reasoned with
As if all of this was history labored on a page
by someone up early
the gold leaf   hours   illuminations   skin
with no obligation
but to say this is thinking   see how exquisite
And then the gold alone
quietly reflecting the grief of phenomena   ecstasy
as if visiting Montana
believing the fiction of pure water   air
filtered of particulates
No uranium   no wondering   nothing but chasing
what doesn't come to you
ignoring what does like being attracted and repelled
like breathing tides
where only the frequency changes as if writing
what might be said
but only to the paper   notebook   the phosphored screen

THE AGE

It was the age. People were getting messages
how to adapt, but they were old messages,
news crossing the ocean on cables, on a steaming raft,
the sky wide open but silent.
Like the out of phase patent on a petrol horse,
a tractor shaped like Dobbin down to the blinders.
The end of one thing leaves its metaphors,
no more gas derived from coal, no whalebone
after steel in m'lady's understructure.
The book in the TV news persists, the candle
still in the desk lamp. And we still have fire with its appetite,
water entering houses like night air up from the creek,
extinguishing nothing, with no comparison and nothing
to improve. The simplest landscape is one straight line.
A touch of brush and a man appears with fire arms,
ocher strikes vermillion, a horse and its enemy,
the future.

at Length

from *NONE OTHER* (2010)

THE NATURAL WORLD

There is no other
To explain where it came from is speculation like reading
water from a faucet. Beyond what we think
in our dreams or ideas it is still there
even the island of walruses.

Inside a house he said
—the man from the rain forest—
inside that Bijoux, Rex, that Paramount, was a hill with steps.
He'd seen it.
And they go up, the whites, the egret people,
they go into the cinema balcony and stare out.
In the dark
ghosts appear on the walls.
Huge people of no substance doing terrible things.
It is death
dreaming on the walls he says.
Back home he will eat only songbirds and howlers
needing their voices to help him
say what happened.

Opening the index I see my list
Chordata
the worm that cries out from its ordered words,
from paper white from oxygen,
type black as onion fields near Sodus, New York,

from centuries of bedrock crumbled together with the old sea floor
things freshly pulled from the earth
and displayed
in neat rows at the roadside stand.

Madame Vidalia, dressed in slips, a seer from below
Russets whose brown skins bake open.
They are protective
if we know their names:
Kingdom   Phylum   Class

Opening Webster's to *estivation*
I thought was a summer sleep, what lungfish do in the dry season,
land snail stuck to the house plaster,
I find it the arrangement of petals within a flower before it opens as well,
and maps of their little inner galaxies,
spiral backbones,
and other names in reverence,
words said softly to the dark:
involute. revolute. obvolute.
convolute. supervolute. induplicate.
conduplicate. plaited. imbricated.
valvate. circinate. twisted. alternative. vexilary.
cochlear. quincunx. contorted.
curvative. equitant.
Nineteen.
By this time none of my friends will be listening.

Imagine a page
orbiting the 320 possible faces of crystals,
ointment from *anoint,*
a scented oil pressed from a flower by a six-fingered hand
from the frieze of posies and ampersands.

Imagine in each train window
that heads are depicted so completely they cannot come loose,
like a traveling exhibition,
each face a moon floating like babies waiting to be born,
moving through the stark cities and ragged yards.

We name durations.
We do not name the shorter disasters:
tornado *Alice,* waterspout *Belle,*
don't name lightnings
or the gust from the chimney dousing the lights.

In Nebraska
another tornado tries to screw something heavenly to the fields
whose rows come together in the theoretical distance.
We hear the wind next door
get caught trying to slip unnoticed through the wind chime.
A reminder
the world insistently presses against us
not like frotteurs on subways or a bus in Rome
but like azaleas the window, the water propping the house up so we'll
notice,
tight as peptides.

We cannot pick blackberries anymore
on the path to The National Seashore
because they spray for mosquitoes even where no one is living.
So many so afraid of nature they send trucks to end it.
If they looked back they might see their own long reluctant shadows
as if dragging their deaths behind.

EARTH SCIENCE

A silence
as when leaving a city the uniting quiet spreads
like the transformational influence of the art of some underdogs.
On a ledge overlooking Arkansas
delicacy is not lost in distance anymore than quartz or olivine
in the crystallization of magma
though you may grow woozy near the edge.
The inadequate is us.
Genetics is like the flurry of Daggers and Prominents
in the halogen death-moons at the Texaco gas plaza in Eureka Springs
calculating quietly without us.

None of this requires a creature self-aware.
No catastrophists. No creationists. No arrogant nations whose rockets
protect them.
No one unfolding the Alps on paper
while wooden structures change quietly to stone.
A couple drawn unwittingly together because of their underbites.
Myths are how one participates
assured the impossible is ours.

The unconvinced
want footnotes a throw rug on the ocean floor   new windows for deflecting
firearms.
Departures from normal are magnetic anomalies.
Finding tireless islands like the cookies from last March still unopened on
the table.

Christmas cards from the year before that. We are accruing a schematic.

The continents are slipping but the older is not farther off

only covered up on the coffee table by *National Geographics*.

Clastics. Synclines.

Fortunes faded and brittle.

Footprints turned to stone.

SOLVING FOR X

Aristotle and his cranky commentators,
Darwin's critics in a dark room like bees dazed by endless clover,
the buffalo down to a few,
the subtracted intimidating sound of wings of passenger pigeons,
a thundering softness, darkening at noon the plains of Kansas,
now a long lost wind in a unique contrivance, uniquely human:
extinction from abundance.

To Hell
with the Argument by Design. Something has gone wrong
down on the planet whose atmosphere swirls like a soapy fever.
The sick animal, earthly in fatigues,
is armed and reloading.
A structured leading edge manages lift from a partial vacuum
and laminar flow.
It contains the strong hollow bone of a bat
or gun barrel.
Some parakeets are thriving in Palm Harbor, some pets flushed,
others let off at the end of the road in another neighborhood.
This is close as we come to solving for X,
a diminishing equation.

To the unknown
and presumptions about them
the propositions are like a concerto in three movements:
Arrow of Time,

which may turn backwards into its flight path
after skewering the target;
Illusion of Equilibrium,
recognized when after dinner overlooking the sunset,
we have to ask who is purring
and what color does arsenic turn in the atmosphere anyway;
and More the Merrier,
which we never believed, in which exuberance and poignancy
fall on the same note, prolonged, prayerful, unheard.

CONSERVATION OF ELEGY

We use *dead* center for bullseye
We like reckless since it sounds like no wrecks
but is dying just the same
Like blasting both our fathers to powder
the process and language denying
what we always said about bodies: keep them care for them
as themselves as ideas
like concentric circles that are guides
ribs in a long dark tunnel.

We like to say *pass on   pass over*
like to say *outtage* like the lights
but we clutter our sky with star hiss and animals
so thickly they cannot

In the backyard earth
the generality we know best about the planet
compost reduces by half
refuse returning to earth in one season
encouraging
the gas-lit grass each blade a perfect stranger
dagger-flames green as envy
all numbers lucky lotto another chance
We are after more
than the usual understanding

LOSING TRACK

They are libraries.
Even the little doily maker is a book itself,
from the book of spiders, a speck that looking at plain air
sees a place in it where silk geometry could fit,
shapes too fine to focus a shadow,
and knows how its snowflake deforms and wobbles
more than 2=XY on the graphing calculator,
how to stay calm
while the threads go limp between the two waving stalks of goldenrod,
and recognize wind that peels bark,
flakes the micro chips of the tempera Last Supper in the damp refectory,
that borrows a book of its own when a dopey looper tingles its feet.

I lose track. The magazine details flutter on my knees
awaiting a check-up.
A blurred figure is swimming in a lighted pool,
then Nigeria drifts past, something in neon, the gas that shivers all night
in its glass letters without fatigue,
the toothed stars that settle in just above the trees in a time-lapse,
a low breath.
And what is whispered splits like a milkweed
and drifts.

I cannot open like the book of wallpaper samples
but learn from those who can
make the crocodiles see-through, show the baby in the kangaroo,
make rats out of shadows,

find a scorpion drifting in the clouds, bones in my clothing on a chair.
And from whom we overlap:
Freud in my father's lifetime, Einstein in mine
a few blocks away on Mercer in Princeton.
Then Hitler for us both, confusions of the inner ear,
a sick swirling.

from *OMNIVORE* (2009)

ANOTHER CONFIRMATION

Annoyances that disrupt the evening news
like gnats that might have
come in with us unnoticed through the French doors
whirling like electrons
remind us the universe starts just above the armchair
its upholstery skin
revealing this metaphor where the cosmos is a body
and the x-rays from quasars
and the strays from Dr. Hinman's side room see
right through us to the slats
and pillows showing we are as continuous with streaks
that scratch the atmosphere as with a slough
of peepers on Discovery saying enchilada to the moon

HOW

How often the boards do not fit together,
how they have been patched, how painted,
how frequently they peel
and the patches often not of the same material,
so a screw must be added or new glue
now separated from the cold,
how nicks are unfinished, wood showing,
how splinters, how the corner of the table is missing
entirely, how the porch settled and the doors
squeaked since and don't close properly,
how caulk, how porcelain, how the pattern
once clipped into hexagons has gaps,
how often we might be described that way—
a house leaning slightly, ever more dependent
on loosening parts on a hill in New England,
lead white above an unrepairable ocean.

ONE HOPED

To make the cosmos seem homelike
ferns revolved like planets on their wires
beauty's exquisite vocabulary hushed
by distance's black glove whose finger
dragged the evening rivers through Arkansas
In such a local universe one hoped
the sky might be encouraged to make up its mind
to rain or shine finally and be done with it
and the moon might give up its neighborhood
and become the water it longed for

THE NEWS

Another fox at the house corner
Another stingray like the Valley of Jehosaphat
Another cloudbank like starched swans
Daylight again busy with its watch and gardening
Night with its Gladstones packed up
The heron the blue one and the several bleached
swim the air banking left against resistance
moisture crowded with mouthfuls
A woman in Florida is asleep between two cardinals
and the news   It cannot last There was a cut-short song
There was another bomb in Ramala   Finally a wren
left its nest in a torn screen when a mower next door
unbelievably started its engine with a string

ORACULAR

In a statistical moment all the horses in Ocala
touched their noses to the grass at the same time.
The odometer rolled to all sevens like a payoff.
A word was spoken in the car and the radio at once.
The sky blue uncountable flowers on hillsides
closed when we heard the gene was found for asthma.
What could be more oracular.
Then picnickers gathered under rest stop overgrowth.
They walked dogs. They ate dogs. They sacrificed in fire.
Smoke showed us turbulent hydrangeas in the air.
Semis flashing their rain ruffles danced tangos.
Sundown held sacred began bleeding in the creek.
A car passed us, then a wide load, then a car again.

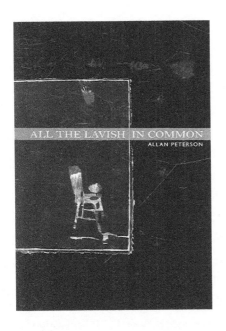

from *ALL THE LAVISH IN COMMON*
(2006)

PRIVATE LIVES

How orb-weavers patch up the air in places
like fibrinogen, or live in the fence lock.
How the broom holds lizards.
How if you stand back you will miss them
afflicted by sunset,
the digger bees mining the yard,
birds too fast to have shadows,
the life that lives in the wren whistle.
You will see moth-clouds
that are moving breaths
and perhaps something like the star
that fell on Alabama
through the roof of Mrs. E. Hulitt Hodges
and hit her radio, then her.
No, you must be close for the real story.
I remember being made
to stand in the corner for punishment
because it would be dull and empty
and I would be sorry.
But instead it was a museum of small wonders,
a place of three walls
with a weather my breath influenced,
an archaeology of layers, of painted molding,
a meadow as we called them then
of repeatable pale roses,
an eight-eyed spider in a tear of wallpaper
turning my corner.
The texture. The soft echo if I talked,
if I said I am not bad if this is the world.

ELEMENTARITY

In the almost unkeepable archives of recall
I think it was Robert Billingsly
who after learning of the muon and meson
discovered the hardon
as both easily detectable and basic and years later
following his bubbles
through a school of silversides off Santa Barbara
large as a car lot
watched how they formed around him a thinking rose
So he added the singular
hard factors of astonishment to his basic elements
and began to imagine
how combinations of these particles might create a world
where venality was not recompensed
deep pleasure was constant and not disgraceful
the ephemeral was eternally resident
though seen glimpsingly and sympathy became common
as silver fish forming an aster
suggesting the appearance of a single mind
So when the car in Clearwater
was pulled over because it appeared to the officer
an iguana was driving
both hands on the wheel though his owner as a prank
had merely slouched down
he thought it was just another extensive etcetera
the charges of which are neutral though nonetheless electric

FROM THE HEART

To say it right you would have to gather the printers of Meriden
Connecticut   and of Basel
paper makers from Twin Rocker   ink grinders   cuttlefish and soy
metalflake   lapis suspended in oil
typecutters calligraphers applicators rubricators floralized reps
from tattoo parlors who are talking pictures
You would use only small letters since you mean soft and intimate
use plain water but natural not tap
that with spat and barnacles   nauplia   zoea   zooplankters   hydroids
more varied than intruding vessels from science fiction
a phrase like pigmy mammoths
two ospreys whose doubles float below them for miles
pidgins   dialects   jargons   creoles
rebus acrostic and seven down the nine letter word for outnumber
Nothing is simple but what we choose to ignore
like the ciliated tufts in the oviducts of a mouse waving like grass
seasonal variations in salinity
If nature is all we have the god-noun that encompasses everything
and I am of it since it cannot be otherwise
then everything I imagine is and   all scrutinized day night or afternoon
on the knobby couch and bumper flash
from Nancy's classic Thunderbird   This is the message:
Of love letters in English there are 26 and feelings outnumber flies

VISCOSITY

You remember poets those that write tangibly
about the intangibles
the way confident water softens red beans overnight
just by conviction,
onions whose pale dresses keep slipping off
despite their shy vegetability,
that provide a planetarium inside a planetarium
where their science sees what's missing
—dark matter—and compares it to a backyard pond
with black mollies so we'll understand;
who were some of the first to notice the sketch
more satisfying than the finished
painting, that dreams induce lightning and the like,
that pages despite desperate messages
turned yellow on the shelves, whether handled or ignored.

Yes to eons, out of print illustrations, yes to the innocent
ginkgos, the confiscated shadows
whereby even in December it is summer by the lamps
and we linger there,
the dust like diatoms in the salty ocean falling slowly,
hanging suspended, laden though they are,
a choir convincing a forest of hands in the molecules
to lift them.
When I first saw Frances in the printmaking studio
at Southern Illinois,
the light shafts began to solidify, the tray of nitric tightened

to its bubbles, the room thickened
and stayed with me.

Now after forty years nothing aromatic has reached the
 ceiling,
nothing then falling reached the floor.
It is the kind of thing like mind and resemblance you'd say
are merely opinions,
but it's still three in the afternoon and she's still turning
younger toward the door.

TODAY THE SWALLOWS

Today the swallows wrote Shakespeare in the air.
          I saw sonnet after sonnet, swooping exeunts, pulled curtains.
Last night a tanager sat learning its wings in my hand.
          It took minutes. Next I was waking
to bells light as feathers.
          So this poem will be a relic layered with sorrow like its kind,
hand over hand, sedimentary accrual the top of which is compromise
with the happy ending, the ceiling, the roof with its wings on downstroke,
the home symbolically leaving,
          so abandonment is an everyday fact encompassing how long
it took to live after it, by which time most have achieved obscurity,
the distance from the sun to its flower, my head whose sutures
are arranged like a comic dawn.

At once the trees were beaded with leaf buds,
          April unbuttoning May.
In no time the empty yard was full, covered over,
          the expanse become a tunnel, plywood turning
framing into walls.
In no time we are convinced we have memories,
          that somewhere the brain records everything,
that timeless often drags on, reasons traced to trees and savannas,
caves and ice-blocks.
At the same time we think ourselves unique, heirs to almost nothing
but blue eyes and hair, dim skin
on which we have pinpricked symbols as reasons, reminders,
          like seeing sky twice, one birdless and empty,
one almost metrically alive.

HOW FAR BEHIND WE ARE

Not just the downbeat and retrieval of the heart,
this developed much earlier and involved the octopus
smart as a dog, Spaniel smart as a pig,
horse smart as a . . . well now you've got me,
maybe the Music Volute printing symphonies outright on its shell.

Stories began to involve someone being two places at once,
having conversations with a broom,
someone showing a gold thigh at Biblos and Tyre
in a single afternoon.

No one ever considered things to be that widespread.
Even arithmologists who value counting, underestimated straw.

Ordinarily the occipital decides, when sunlight makes a face on water
and the wind draws in a beard and wild hair,
or you sit in a dark room and stars assemble their oncoming Pontiacs.

We are hungered by images.
We feed mutually after we make them.
We can comb out the face with our thoughts,
make out maps to a treasure on the wings of a Checkerspot.
We gather the animals dressed in flowers and music,
we open their throats since they do not pretend higher purpose.

This is how far behind we are. Our mysteries. Our little ignorance.
Rituals made of nothing but surprise,
as when gardenias burn in one's presence just by touch.

AN ANECDOTE

sounds like a cure for something
but is a little revelation
like mute one morning after the stroke he woke up
to see all the children
flown in with nieces nephews interchangeable husbands
and uttered his first words
O my goodness
suddenly knowing it was downhill from there.
When I went out the back door
of the last room at Lake Quinault into the hillside forest
of salal and discovery
and found signs and markers identifying trees
and native vegetation
it was like a family gathering. There was a danger
of losing everything.
I should have taken Raymond Bluefield a local to tell me
the names and how Miriam
his daughter was spoken to by spiders how the elk appeared
as his father to say he was leaving
for good for the Olympic forest how in his double-ender
now he feels like Mary of the Moon
and I might say stop. Pay no attention to the rest.
Sometimes Blue Jays will scold us
to the whole outdoors though we are only refilling the
     feeder.
The real details are the unexpected
taking on new life. None of us can tell when children gather
or leave or where or what we may do
with our intentions our useless medicine at the last minute.

BONE STRUCTURE

Lint is the end of things, and bones, algae and refusal
to accept new evidence of the last world or the next.
    Fish bones, a puzzle of shatters like broken glass,
a clock impossible to wind or rebuild without parts left over,
mirror images of *no* and *on,* a spine cascading like a flight of stairs.
    Every bone with its dark-finned shark process swimming
relentlessly through daylight.

Now the Willet with the limp is back
after escaping the Sharp-shinned. Now there are pen lines for veins
and unequal footprints, water copying their eyes.
    Now the landscape is long breaths and nine muscles
enter quietly the thumb, the lace of the chain link
beautifies the lawn.
    Now the dancer who was a jeweler by day
and the gemstone that was a dancer by night, are waiting
for coils to vermillionize the stove.
Who will speak first of the fall of '85. How many objects
remind them of time lost to each other, limbs lost, letters.
-A- with its legs widespread, -F- with its ligatures.

    And the falls since, each recollection paying for shadows
on the white page, cream page, bone between,
white only by comparison and favoring one leg,
    shifting weight, uneasy in dead silence.
Behind them the Coldspot was dropping its ice cubes
    like femurs and phalanges out of danger
behind the sturdy and insulated door.

TRESPASS

The recent was so enough, I quit.
What more was there, anyway.
As it is in Arkansas, so it is in English,
but the outcomes are more complicated.
The arc of minutes in the sky over Hot Springs
left plenty. So much, I decided, was self-evident.
For instance, one lung is smaller than the other.
The reason is the heart
which is not quite middle, but the left.
The same side on which I hear superior.

In reading "The Illustrated Wasps of Ireland,"
I heard our shared wrens so loud I sat
bolt upright into the loads of listening.
Which is more pathetic, those winged children,
innocent infants of the times, or horoscopes,
whose front pages equal the news of Zambia
or Bonn.

Dragging out the photographs of Mao
swimming the Yangtze,
he has been there so long without moving
he must be puckered beyond belief.
So answer the telescope, ring up the distant
and disharmonious families. You see our problem.
There are so many of us now, and we are lying.

VIRTUES

Because William Tell was just a remake of Abraham and Isaac
and both lucked out out of arrogance and obedience
because all flowers are black at night and the object-lesson sons
who were only ideas about whose is whose and how much one is
willing to lose for the sake of sheer instruction   Do as I say or else
Like they liked to repeat in art school about a given composition
how the eye is *led* like a puppy from the cup to the window
to the painter with the rolled newspaper
Out the window we think there is a globe tugged on by a moon
but the lake does not move under it   It is still there in the corner
of New Hampshire The daylight itself is swallowed every afternoon
at the far end red as an apple poured down a throat like mulled cider
None of it is true Were we doing as we were told already   Or can it
happen without a threatening example of gaining by almost losing
Just by the grip of realizing you are capable of holding the knife yourself
The real terror may be daylight and night dreams merely a rest from it

BREATHING WITHOUT EXHALES

This is unbearable we say while doing just that,
reading our lips as if the shapes settled like letters,
like waxwings on a branch baseline.
Nothing is lost from the lines or the photographs.
No amount of reading wears them away, lips or no lips,
jambs or iambs looking so similar in lower case.
The cathedral is upheld, stone humming, ribs vaulting,
insinuation and insulation at the same time.
Credo, I believe, and dado, how meaning interlocks
with stones as the birds settle into the limestone cornice.
Some things inside-out as Gothic, outside-in as socks,
wrong-sided Red-winged blackbird, Black-winged
red bird, tanagers the idea-mirror is held up to.
Las alas, las olas. I write out love to you in flying words,
leaving like water. It settles on my hand on your hip.
I can hardly stand it I say while standing it.

HOLDING YOUR HORSES

In missing there is a sense like hearing a faint sound
almost lost like a key turning in buckshot down a hall
I presume an internal sense of completeness
in all things as much for Jan Jackson as for her horse
whose time on the vet's table was a dream
with one flat side   The doctor said it was perforated
and leaking like a tea ball urgent and in Latin

Waking in her room between sleep and gas bills
she saw a bare leg stick out from the covers
like a bloodless fracture   In her dream she had just
    moistened
two fingers and pinched a wick and the light had fizzled
into a tendon that became the close end of one of the
    muscles
of the night that whinnied and flexed in its field
and though not surviving ran again in its new dark pasture
coming to no one   not for apples   not for oats

LASTING IMPRESSIONS

Look at the slight valley of the horse between haunch and shoulder,
recalling its rider and the low hills between. Form never forgets.
Though they are free to be real horses not obscured by work,
not pull anything, they must think hard to do nothing but remember
their lovers to run the low hills and dream and eat up green landscape.
He thinks of her and the way part of him still sinks down the cushions
when he's gone. A few remembering shapes linger till the foam or feathers
take a deep breath and remember what they were. If he comes back soon
he may not be quite missing, indentations rising as if still getting up.
When he leaves he feels her still on him, a loving cinch like the feel of hat,
the hat gone.

HOW FOLKLORE STARTS

It was during the year when masterpiece was not impossible
but increasingly unlikely—this one—when I heard the announcer
say William Berg's Mass for Three Horses instead of three voices.

At the time I thought, fabulous, this could turn everything around.

The beautiful oven of the August Gulf is seen best from Wisconsin.
Too much hot metal to touch, too many hopes heaped on impossible,
the clippings of which are faded and worn through from your wallet.

A good title but hopeless when I heard them actually harmonizing
not like horses at all, but rhymes like little bells ringing in words
to no purpose but attention to themselves, scaffolds, not Appaloosas.

What more could be done to prepare that story.

After currying, grooming, dressing for dinner in new shoes,
something swirls offshore in overheated uncertainty. You can hear hooves
in the gathering clouds, pawing to begin, a fugue in alternating names.

TRIAL

Nothing more poignant than a being trying
to understand itself,
than a being helping another with no understanding
other than need, nothing more
than a being knowing something, caring for something
incapable of care,
than one caring for knowing so that care might be
available when needed,
when need is not wonder but a being itself.

Our myths were Indians though this was not India.
We ruined them obsessively.
Now farms. We crush the small ones and poison
the larger, all wistlessly.
In the jurisdiction of humiliation we are peerless.
Magniloquent. Eating our own.
In dislike and loathing are no honeymoons.
A man covered in bird feathers, a field feathered with corn.
Each could overcome us
and so defeat endless successions of threats,
endemic to out of date worlds.

The arid climate of exclusion rots leather armor.
Shock strikes quietly.
Aiders and abettors are conspicuously forgiven.
The rooftop would be opened like tent flaps,
legends rewritten in the fields.

Black water would argue against us.
Enter the alkaloids.
Enter water and electrolytes.   Too much and too little.
Causality going one way, morality the other,
hiding their eyes.

CRITICAL MASS

Take a place like Horseheads New York named for remains,
transformed from a once peaceful location to carnage,
or people under-experienced, but in famous ways. Gary or Florence,
maybe average students in Oregon or Indiana. We've forgotten.
Today I picked *pools* instead of *leaves* from the screen-saver
and chose nine knots of complexity that made the Nile brown,
then red, then cyanotic, followed by the longest lace-edged
meander in extraordinary rose.
There are so few great ideas, so many mediocre, or worse,
the average collects until catcalls asking next door for Friskies
become shouts: a sudden whirlwind of migrating arrivals
and the extraordinary children with rhyming names, loose horses
looking for their mythical fathers in the sea, extra gold eyes.
I know I remember so much more just by being in the yard.
Each thing reminds me stories by their presence: centipede ferns,
the loved dog coiled in the ground story, the bat tree unknown
till we cut it down,   wasp dragging a spider who couldn't lift it
and couldn't let it go,   mantis eggs,   her unforgettable dress
put aside by the sea wall,   all the lavish in common.

RELUCTANT

The body is never out of style,
      unlike some frescoes in Bologna.
The earth never stops roasting and freezing by turns.
There are always the poles of diaphysis
and epiphysis of the long bones, for those who have them.
      Reluctant to let go, we might try on a funeral
or two as a last chance.
If we can't keep the body, maybe just the heart
like Egyptians in small jars.

And maybe by staring one might see a wisp
lighten the body, as dreams may evaporate
from the muscleless condition of paradoxical sleep,
      that the portion of the horse we are born with,
cauda equina, might be set free in the pasture,
while the rest of the body is removed by the back door,
serenely and with flowers,
      perhaps painted and dressed atmospherically,
as might Masaccio.

UNDER OATH

When my grandfather, who had only the day before
axed the head off a chicken
and let it run ragged till dead dry in the driveway,
came at me with a switch
on a dead run, shouting blood as I was playing pioneer
and axing with an oar the young maple he planted,
I saw between strokes the end of imagination,
and would have said it then, but was struck dumb:
I'm sorry. I promise
to abandon the ground level fixity of purpose,
making things worse. I promise
to undo the mildewed grout of the worse for wear,
to improve from erosion, corruption, gangrene and
    mischief.
I promise to reform North America,
profess the inheritability of guilt and sorrow for Hiroshima
that will come later in '44,
regardless of who prevails militarily. I promise
on the stellar interiors, mitochondria, ionized trails
in the atmosphere, the galvanized tub as my wading pool.
I promise not to misuse the past or the future
if I should have one.

WHAT BELONGS

If you take them by thousands from Suriname
or the orange backrivers of Asia, they will continue in your aquarium,
but diminished, as bad news we come to think novel or quaint.
Not oblivious to place, they are merely unable to tell you
they shouldn't be there, and you can't see it.
I am thinking of the pink pearly Arawana in the New Orleans restaurant
that moves slowly like a pennant in oil, too long furling in the light,
every motion beautifully deliberate and prolonged. Its trail lingers
like the tail behind a flashlight searching for whereabouts,
lost and irretrievable. Or the lionfish, splendidly ragged reef ivy,
bluer the deeper, but seven within twelve miles
right in the middle of the Florida Panhandle, one in the window
between pizza and discount clothes. In this, self- indulgence has bypassed
respect, distilled wonder to novelty. They are only small dollars
like Discus from Brazil. They move like the caged in perpetual U-turns
and ovals, the sad shapes of captivity. These are immoral and excessive times.
Even the moths that live here openly throw themselves willfully
and desperately against the lights.

COSMOLOGY

Ok, there was the sky woman and the earth man,
there was the original snake and the three fire stones,
stars as a river and strewn coals;
there was everything from nothing, from three or four
elements to more than a hundred with the theoretical
metaphors of shepherds from herding peoples,
fish from fishers,   kings from cats,
world as a flat circle with a bowl over it marked with stars,
figures of the dead watching for failures;
there was the monkey in a tree that came down
to be us on the grand savannas
that gave us sore backs,   the couple in a garden asked to
     leave
from some of the same presumptions of innocence
and ignorance,
all the stories of something using a language with no words
for what it really is, or even that you could know it,
determine the true past from here,
that whatever we suggest, there is always something
behind it, or beside it, or many at the same time. Mythology
is a caster for the mind, a cushion like a rubber cup
under the sofa to protect the floor.
That is why we can't get there, why sacred and scared
are anagrams of each other.

SAD FACTS

From the unmistakable garden of good reasons
for inventory to become narration,
the azalea opens its corolla to the flies and spiders,
the dogwood gives up its denizens:
wood borers, tongue worms, ants.

Children heal quickly as they do everything.
As for the rest of us,
our wounds are remarkably low in oxygen,
high in traumatic acids.

The person unable to write anything may sing,
explaining what is damaged.
The stutterer sings. The heart murmurs,
then speaks. The words are recorded.
There are gaps and glitches in the tapes.

If the words are changed the landscape withers.
We will have no nostalgia for the farm.
We will separate like seeds and cease believing.
We will stand back telling two stories at once,

how things in good order are anxious for tomorrow,
how some things do not continue, cannot
as corn cannot reseed without us,
increasing the list of things we have made helpless.

And what of this: the calf in the pasture
that became a flowered purse, a shoe.

TRANSFUSION

I have written it five times or more, each uneasy.
Drafts, as if wind blew uncomfortably through and the loose door chattered,
the toilet spoke with its moan voice, the deep pipes shuddering.
After a long wait trying to remember his name,
I touched the phone book and it came without opening.
I felt a chill.
Then I wondered the whereabouts of the South Star
since a North existed and touched the Ephemeris. Nothing. No one had.
Another symmetry misspoke.
And for the second time Terry's own blood left the table,
swirled through the room and tubing before return.
Imagine its migration in a single room,
petrels in the blood from far away as South America.
After the machinery it came back.
You could hear it like the whump of wind refilling sails to the shapes of
    colters
on the way to the self-centered idea of the New World,
well new to some Spanish.
But it was the same world, now in miniature, the masts relaxed
in their neck rings, then teased up on ropes like a path to the Western Ocean
which was the Eastern Ocean
through a miracle of circuitry and cruelties.
In the last draft the patient became an explorer through his blood
which traveled in pinwheels though he stayed put, whirlpools,
all aspects of weather on a sphere which revels but does not survive,
and the story almost unrecognized from where it started.

WITNESS TO INCREASING PERIL

Eric our checker has Conformity
Is Suicide tattooed
on his forearm as a footnote for life.
He rings up the lemons
and bouquet and flashes his attitude
in flesh text
while under him his shadow makes fun.
First a rhino as he swipes.
A dwarf sideways behind his back.
Traditional fluorescents working against him.

There is nothing in the myths anymore
just this over and over.
And there is conformity. There is witness
to increasing peril.
There is spending just to go fast. Double-bagging
opinionated hopes.
But no energy's left in the Don't Look Back,
the ruined man
twisted to a stick, waking up from death
like a nap mistaken,
the always assumption of Something More,
especially for us.
And if you have it,   what do you have.
And then what.

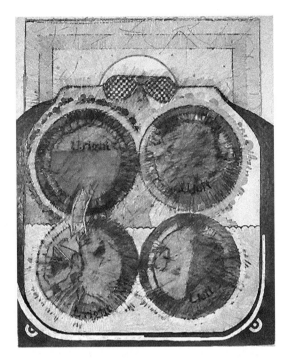

from *ANY GIVEN MOMENT* (2005)

REVELATION

Yanking smilax I received the gardener's stigmata

a thorn through leather

and found at the mailbox the rabbit like referred pain

one side skinned by impact

The anatomist foxes took it the first night

I then saw a fisherman offshore

and before he made it bait by the steel hook

he lifted his arm to show me

and a silversides frantically swam in his hand

TURNING TO JULY

Blue Jays flash down like pieces of Gulf Stream
and drink from the pie plate. You can't make us out
from the many salt water edges or the road.
On eclipse day thousands of hidden cameras
slip their efforts through the leaves and the acre
is littered with moons bitten exceedingly.
I turn the calendar to July a long blue lake in China.
While waiting for October three landsats away I peek.
It's the enormous Mississippi from the sky
where toward the bottom at the Gulf someone unseen
picks up the dipsy worm through their bare feet.

EMBOLI

Seeds were more trustworthy than he expected,
generously bringing up things not planted:
candyweed, violets, skullcaps—opportunity's
host to diversity.
Then there was grievance. The azalea died, magnolias
browned as if tourniquets strangled their branches.
When the gardener went white, you couldn't tell him
from gulls or the fiberglass Hatteras,
the clot black as the nerve in this pencil as I write.

PSYCHODRAMA

Today a woman in frustration

spoke to a gas pump

and it spoke back saying depress the lever

and try again

So she told it how things went bad for her

confiding an anger so deep

that nearby sparrows startled and departed

from the looming sign

that said Goodyear with the flying foot

FALSE STARTS

She said false starts. I heard *false stars*.
Like runners that begin and have to come back
because of someone too anxious.
Even if I started now I'd never get there.
It's too far and we can't believe that long.
We'd have to come back.
And they *are* false. They've told us for years.
They may fall right out of the sky while we watch.
They may not even be there now, the light's so old.
Silent light. An old unbelievable song
the farther back you go.

WHITE CHAIRS OVER

The storm last night in its overbearing way

talking too loud throwing things around

turned the white chairs over as if we'd left

for the summer and forgotten the protocol

the slipcover forgotten to unplug appliances

remind our belongings of our lasting affection

for them that we would return to handle them

again saying our secrets in their presence

showing them our bodies

from *ANONYMOUS OR* (2002)

RIGHT BEFORE YOUR EYES

It doesn't take a disaster.
Your life is always passing before your eyes, and through,
as radar through clouds, reshaping into beasts and boulders,
amazing forests, under them sorrowing lawns
in the Western penchant for grass.
Elephants, once clouds in India,
were condensed out of mythology by curses of a holy man.
Now they are among us as we wait to exit the sedimentary
    epoch
of wars, if someone will curse us sufficiently.
It seems possible.
Today for the first time I saw a Carolina mantis,
though they are the most common, against the flat desert
color of the house. I would have missed it on oak bark,
itself a mystery, on which all the plurals are confused,
the opposite of martyred.
And in that blessing I share a great secret.
I know she laid eggs on the phone wire, more between the
    steps.
Little grey clouds in the battle to be both hidden and alive.

THE SOLIPSIST AT NIGHT

The hard to get going days,
like the blood-loaded mosquito leaving my wrist,
running to take off, cannot rise.
If asked color, the depressed might answer black,
sensing the breakdown of hemoglobin,
as iron trying to memorize last night,
becomes merely impudent water that once had dreams.
As night in its black sheath with pearls,
the socialite, the one recently bitten,
or the flowered blood itself loaded with smoke
in the insect apparatus,
swirling with messages, lightens and lifts
or is smacked flat,
or lies hardening to calculi. Who knows.
It is so easy to confabulate the dark,
to be bad or better there for differing reasons;
sounds of the air's black fabric,
wavelets shuffling dark cards, slabs for memorials
quarries from its walls.
From somewhere a fan's excessive breaths,
hearing the drawers of consequence open and close,
hurricanes looking the other way, inward.
The files of excuses, miles
of presumable families anxiously waiting,
anxious black under them.
The solipsist will say yes, I have this,
but what can I know of you, treading water with a look.
What can you know of me, a disharmony of things

EPIGRAPH

Within the epiphyte, the epigraph of a surviving oak
after hurricane Erin, I hear claws,
small ones you'd have to describe by scurry instead of climb,
caused by intention, by fear, caused by who knows what,
a patterned self-saving conclusion in the meat-ribbons,
neat as Vesalius, as a Japanese figure of strip-bamboo and
    grasses
standing on a hill overlooking Hokkaido,
clever and wistful in the eyes.
So much more of the world can fit in by looking down
the wrong end of the Bausch and Lombs,
and adding the one little wiggle before the s that means
    possession
at the end of every word. Accretion, fly paper, taking itself
as fact in the interconnection of all things,
brain meat mediating not greedily, but serene.
It is easy to dream or visit Disneyland, both synonymous
with surreal, and then write outlandishly.
There is plenty around in plain facts stuck to each other,
flying squirrels gliding and scrambling, each finger-needle
another idea for the bark, a little inward light as in August I
    dive in.
The ocean glows. I swim to the sandbar, a ladder of
    illumination,
self-healing lights, a scratchy quote above the waves.

BECOMING WHAT YOU CAN

The five-rayed hand occurs with some frequency.
A hardened and pointed face often shoots out
like a thrush or curlew. One applauds the other.
The man in the outboard pulls up a long possibility
followed by gulls. His hand on the net rope took ages to
    occur,
so many they are named, not numbered.
The rope that raises blisters is a thread that disappears
through deep history to the end and a lost button, the
    fingers
of the future would twist in the eyelets,
small and unthinkable from here.

A hand appears in the flipper of a seal. A beak longer
in a thrush in a single generation. A tuna at the end
of a long line of tuna. There is no Final Accounting.
It is all Becoming. Even the little deathshop of history
stays open all night and the patrons repeatedly disappear
from their houses, their boats. Now the phalanges
are so few they are numbered not named
and the bonewhite tern suspends in one place above a
    minnow,
and this action is changing the future: proximal, medial,
distal as the focus of the unhurried yet to be.

THE SHORTCHANGED SHADOW

Never enough details to fill it out,
like insects with the hyphenated waists,
the grapefruit moon that cannot be recognized
chopsticked by trees. The shadow is no news,
only lingering regret, side-lighted.

If we had not seen the white pelicans spell
out the future by rewinding clouds,
it would have meant telling the storm by sand,
or plumage by ankles of the oaks
where the deer find lichens.

Identity is open to interpretation,
so is not identity at all. In many cases
we have not come to the end of what
things might be, as with the descriptions
of her back: a tree lushed by trapezium,
symmetrical spatulas, hangers for landmarks
and double hands.

We are so bad at knowing
where one leaves off and another begins,
as if meaning was only pale remains,
as when losing water to the air, grass shrivels
like burdened joy exceeding one's oranges.

FROM NOW ON

A force like water turns the mill wheel.
A cocktail of current turns the dream.
But that is useless now.
No one remembers a mill wheel and dreams
are described as random activity,
hearts more turnips than Valentines.
Frances is awake and beating the organic mattress flat
to take back what it borrowed of her body overnight.
Things sap us while they work,
so no more sweet descriptions of flowers as flames,
even though the azalea is burning inside the window.
No more sanding my knees looking for shark teeth,
though sleepless oceans thrash the shore.
I will try harder than water.
I will be telling you the worst.

DISTANCE LEARNING

Ray has taken his lawn chair to the boat
hoping to call a redfish to the chaise like a string telephone.
If he is successful we can learn something.
How the infinite is merely more than one can imagine,
therefore a commonplace.
What feels like barn door is a halibut, a man
connected to deep reluctance with a ruffle.

Botticelli's model for the *Birth of Venus*
was a cousin of the Amerigo America was named for.
You'd think a Neoplatonist could have just drawn
a woman up from past experience
by opening the memory of responsive forms.
We say we know from faith and legend,
but such connections are always unexpected
as if a pleading mantis should receive a voice.

WHAT BESIDE A BIRD

Double take of the ordinary fears.
Each day burning to black ash beyond the bay bridge.
The surprising shortness of her skirt.
But on hearing the friend she just saw Tuesday
did not survive the hospital
the door to incongruous contexts dropped from its hinges.
Ginger said she'd always been told the worst thing
was dealing with the death of a horse.
Sometimes harder than people. Her horse is thirty.
Something about their muscularity and size.
How hugely they carried the human spirit in every culture
they touched.   What beside a bird we want to be
brings home the immensity of death.
You must have several things in order. First where, she said.
Who will put her down in the final euphemism.
All steps readied, the place decided:
off in the pasture under the willow, the pecan for her color,
in your chest where the hollow is
already widening between husband, children, and friends,
where you can't look back,
where attraction shrinks stunned before care.

BLUE ANGELS

Carol says Beth is more interested in primates
growing as we do backbones first
while she is more orchids and palms In the Amazon
the utmost West parades them both
They blossom as the blossom of shadows between them
the warm and warmer fortunate long straws of light

Today the Blue Angels are practicing
You'd think it would have come naturally
but these are not the real thing only our mechanical
        examples
singing portions of our nerves back to us
Because we are geniuses each paddle leaves an aster in the
        river
Howlers send down vanilla from the trees

For the atheist heaven is the earth
What I hear it say is heard better with the left ear
remembered better with the right
I hear the five blue jets blossom like petals at the heart of
        timing
I recall how closely one travels with the disaster of belief

DARK COMPANIONS

A flutter of something far away
a city   a star whose own wings interrupt its light
a variation suggesting a dark companion

And here is the kingfisher
dark star itself   not fifty yards off flickering
above itself   seeing through glitter to the minnow

Yesterday on the anniversary of Nylon
Ganymede was described in new photos
as looking like thin ice

a place where you skate alone at great risk
where you see ghost shapes in the greeny glaze
Below you history is described as panorama

but experienced as single poignancies
discrepancies probably not to be resolved
But I hate to say never

hate to say a feather is like dead hair
to stand back and see less detail than before
I know they have thumbs and fingers

the birds variously interrupting the planets
the cities whose ribs open to the twin tricksters
day and night

I know any minute a thrasher
standing on the frozen birdbath will try drinking
with the gauzy bird beneath it

HAVING PLANETS

The numbers which suggest an unattainable atmosphere,
Drake's equation expressing the likelihood of a star
having planets, subtractive light in the lowermost eyes,
the problematic oxygen and the halving of abundance
in various models of evolving alkaloids to eliminate pests,
are being calculated on my window by a stinging rain.

Meanwhile, sunlight is alive on the napkin rings,
those silver, those bone. And the table is a model
of an orderly universe given the moon plates arrangement,
place-cloths like those of magician's devices for obscuring
the trick but deafening the eyes, hiding the hands.
And glass for the oceans, the water hardened into geometry,
the squid-fork, protozoan spoons, and the entirely absent
arguments for reliable first causes, let alone last.

Such improbabilities are more likely at close range,
the eggs breathing, vibrations of our inner neighborhoods,
invariants we can grasp, the sugared promises
amidst the infuriating architecture of our slow and porous
conclusions. During dinner the tendencies toward stability
enlarge. Local is what we know slightly, just as the distant,
and our smallest assumptions orbit the entire like debris.

SIDEREAL LIFE

The instance is the right hand, the knee bone
in orbit within the dark garden,
sky like a toad skin glittered with chemicals.
Nightmares call me as daydreams for later
on their elder legs. Awake, I write life
in the paper according to hints from the universe.
Memory's a sieve, an old screen
through which squirrels and rat snakes pass
to make trouble in the rafters. Only yesterday the act
of recalling my grandmother whose gallstones sat
on the dresser with her combs, swept decades off the porch.
I cannot read in such dimness, slight as stars,
or stick to the subject. I am tracing my skin against the
    window,
getting graphs instead of landscape.
I am using "a hundred times" to mean many, no matter
how often I address the same questions, familiar
as if they were neighbor's dogs, the light and the dark
I love yous, the twinkling seasons, the farm animals
through which history is written in small pails and chains.

CENTRAL HEAT

There were not even instruments, there was earth.
Weather was a visitor, climate resided.
Tightrope snow on the powerlines was the last Vaudeville
before barometric depressions
and Peter moved South from Trinity with his silver whales;
Mary stared into her fireplace for months.
Concerned about the dubious ambitions of the notes,
icicles tingling like bells, glaciers, crackling wax,
gyres in the Gulf closing from weariness,
spiders opening their own, we rest on natural appetites.
Once Mexico was water and the oceans dry land.
On the whirling earth, wishing is reckless and untoward.
Things nosedive without our help.
Passing through Panama, I want to say isthmus
without sticking, want hot water to interfere with clouds,
I want rings around the moon.
We should have expected a cold climate, tornadoes moving
    north.
Only one third of the Gulf Stream is Gulf, the rest is
    deflection.
This is how migration began, anticipating the long
    established
deep usefulness of ruin.

FOUR GONE CONCLUSIONS

One that the newsreels might be different the second time.
That after the moon evaporates, the ocean
will finally make up its mind and come in for good, but kindly.
The river at Quincy will be passive as hypoglycemia
as it eats the shore every summer
and will not start turning the farmhouses back into boards.
That the lynchings at Marion Indiana might never have happened.
The crowd at the court house only an extraordinary number
of people seeking a breeze on a hot night.
James Cameron would speak and everyone would listen
till it hurt to the soothing gusts of his words,
and Singapore might be a musical city like its name.
A small someone, maybe Karen Dickenson,
who lived out beyond the city limits, might have held up her hands,
a slipper shell on each finger tip, as if a girl became a gecko
in front of everyone. And after these miracles
everyone would have gone home peaceful and marveling.
But in some situations no forgiveness is possible,
as in this version, the one that really happened.

SKIN

Almost an acre of epidermis can be grown
from a single foreskin
some of the result of which was used on him
at the Booneville clinic
and sometimes the news comes together with the wonder
was it true stars
could be seen in daylight at the bottom of a deep tunnel
and like Homer Freeman
you might imagine losing your balance while your dogs
walked the well-lip easily
and wait two hours with a broken shoulder till Ina Mae saw them
and called the fire trucks
and winches and how he developed a better understanding
of the chapters on arcturus and gravity
and the one-way travel of his animals the cow's long fall to St. Louis
without returning
and what if no one had heard him or saw the dogs
and how he would not be able to say as an aside there was nothing
but darkness with a clear blue eye
that covered him and became the largest organ of his body
surprising as the elm that reached out for lightning or the boy
that ran away from the circus to home

THE CEILING AT ITS WORD

Pink clouds loll in our attic.
      There is nothing like such low heavens.
They are real and the galaxies lost
      in pine stay close enough to hear through the drywall,
tape, and the textured ceilings.
Sometime there will be a sound like water poured on tiles,
sometimes we will empty the dishwasher
and all the local believable moons,
months to come, can be stacked according to magnitude:
saucers, demitasse, dinner the migrators tell by.
      And we can mention over coffee
how we pass over Little Rock, not Hot Springs.
And between the underseasons, between living and sleeping rooms,
      the floor lamp, end table and strenuous existence,
how we reuse them, the long relationships of paths in the rug.
While the wind spends more on the coast than it needs to,
we take the reassuring ceiling at its word.
The earth comes apart like an orange. We are largely protected
      from blindness: moon, night, snow,
and with you under the vigilant fan there is a saving gift
for me like wheat to Egypt.

ABRACADABRA

Water hides water.   Underwater crying is unknown.
I watched the pulsing bullet of the bobbin holder
that worked magically under the silver footplate of the treadle Singer,
timed between the needle like a heart,
binding the disparate together, cloth to cloth.
Inconspicuously tying a knot in the interim.
A pattern of rhyming lines, the magic of which is a triangle
complicated by the paired notions of rust and denial.
Even the movie reviewer in the reindeer sweater said *reduced* to emotion,
meaning getting *down* to such lesserness,
how the scenes like a spell had him, self-consciously, weeping in his seat.
In the ring of people a voice brings a so-called message from the dead,
from whom all news is inconsequential:
Evie, do you recall the nickel in the black purse?   Yes, from the audience.
And the medium John Webber rises above them in Albert Hall.
The photo shows no thread. In another, there is ectoplasm
streaming from his mouth looking suspiciously like a handkerchief.
This happens normally, being suddenly there
in the mirror across the room, then gone as fast.
Counting. Wishing. Calling.   Making faces at the apes.
Expecting something fabulous to happen just by words.

TROPICAL DEPRESSION

How wide is it, the worse for wear, dread we expect,
an avenue marked by its stuttered yellow, almost bones,
civilian as insect pests, blood pressure
adding to the color of its eyes.
Daylight is a pinched pink this early, moist-throated
and moving south out of a disturbance in the Gulf
bearing a name and clothed in various aspects of hiding
by its disguise, wide action, huge shoes,
spinning off children like Quetzalcoatl breathing life
into a skeleton, flowering shinbone, luminous arrows,
face in the altwater swirling off Mexico, frosted with clouds.

Of the real lost software, these are they, long before radar,
the loaded slogans, named for alternating genders. We speak
of their destruction, rooms in the west where they dissipate,
dragged like magnets to a restful end, unpacked.
Who can answer the half tractable. Who expects weather
to wind up in your yard name-calling, the only recently
    decided
coalescing over hundreds of miles into a mission from
    Africa
to uproot your tree through a conspiracy of smudges
and dark turmoil gone green in the weather picture,
a strange caldera. And the point of today and yesterday,
telling shrinkage from expansion, though not enough
to make amends, expecting the tangle, obscuring the origins
of pleasure, and of storms.

DON'T GET ME WRONG

O that.
Something just sheared off another moon-piece that's all—
like what happened to the island.
Probably one of those sky disputes we've heard about.
Those full speed boats are asking for trouble
right after the hurricane. There are whole towns now
under the waters.
Brass props have broken right and left.
The pieces like moon parts lying all over. It's dangerous
as running through the house with sharp objects.
We hear groupers now live among couch pillows
and a shark was seen from a second floor
pulling down little high-fat meals of cormorants .

I know
I am just my history and yours and more or less
everyone's and I do what I can.
My course is influenced by the underground rivers
that explain the spring and the appearance
of watercress smack in the middle of Oklahoma.
I think Vermeer's lacemaker is crafting a neural net
with the tools they had. Colored threads
like we use for coming and going to the heart.
The sky is a relative but this is extinction.
In making we externalize a secret.
We discover how little we arrogantly are,
how often the planets shatter.

FULL OF SURPRISES

Words are not the world they said, and believed it.
They influence others.
So the beat is not the heart for them, those few minutes
of arrhythmia,
its two words stringing out artificial phrases,
a tiresome orthodoxy
describing gaps between meaning and a truth,
sinkholes in the landscape of happiness,
a world, but not this one.
So when I say Frances at night and my heart
triggers the room as she moves closer,
is there any world elsewhere but this.

We do not have a limit to the known. We have noises
coming and going beneath the door,
the visible disappearing with the wavelength of light
in the Zeiss eyepiece.
Birds are dictating essays but when we transcribe them
we have foolishness, *cheek cheek* or a peevish *cheee*
so they may be right.
But there are exemplary types of reason, language
that articulates the wrist: flexion,
extension and the others in fistfulls:
abduction, adduction, flowers puckered shut
as if alum were the air.
And below this the underthumping, one breath

perfecting the next when I see you, and I encourage
the pony in my chest ridden by vision,
small moths adrift in the window corners
with dust and the odd hair.
This is where I want to say surprise.

LEAST OF OUR WORRIES

Forest hawks have short wings to maneuver through trees.
In astronomy we are less fortunate,
wings are useless in a vacuum.   One can hunt nothing,
but that nothing usefully viewed
is only another unrehearsed unknown.
Like the amount of dark matter in the universe,
the mouse of evening,
we can confirm its opportunities, we can see aircraft disappear
in it like a ring in pudding,
we can look at the light and leap to conclusions like a Cooper's
on a squirrel.

On the trip, Marrah kept seeing each distant bird a Snail Kite
since they hadn't seen one but were in its territory.
Such is the urge to discover and confirm,
want striking experience blind.
In school, each of the cupcake papers was an island in the archipelago
we studied, blue foil the ocean.
We had to imagine an inferno acting like hydraulic brakes
where expanding pressure, though neutral, took revenge
slamming upward as the Chevy slowed.
Magma breached the mantle and I saw the earth adrift in a thick cape
like stories from Old Europe, courtiers of planets,
a carriage like a caravel arriving at a new shore, blue awnings in tow.

from *SMALL CHARITIES* (1994)

The farther you go
the model the landscape
the five persimmons
all grow small and change
color on purpose
Art is a diminishing experience
pencils get smaller brushes
unbristle and by the time
Frances saw the Pope
he was a child's thumb
in front of St. Peter's
She could smear him
put out the sun with her hand
touch spires of the ancient city
Not a single splinter
would break off

Needles deep in my room
will me *rain* or *clear*
even with the windows covered
A silver line says hot and however
far that is from normal
Right now I am explaining to myself
the comfort of these signs
I am holding my sharp fingers
to my wrist and counting My heart
is doing a most important addition
Every stair assures me
there is somewhere else to go

Mockingbirds a pair
who though they can sing
with every songvoice and then some
scold this morning unmusically
& must day Honey let's fly down
and eat some of the blood-dark berries
of the wild bamboo and shit them
on the Toyota
I think they say that
because that is what they do

Summer borrows your water
winter your breaths in little smokes
so that death accumulates
in the total of small charities
Some birds drink and are attacked
it seems by something in the water
After a struggle they escape
but return again to that risk
that draws together the birdbath
the Serengeti and the Plain of Jars

What is outside the house is trying
to enter through the windows
to fill up space with itself
as it has the compost now a network
you could lift as a single shape
more roots more branches shadows

the throwaway parts of trees
Out and inside an inch different
you almost can't know them apart
as one gives way to the other
but the window sweats at the danger
As I reach down to plant the balled dogwood
in the dog hole I see roots
have already entered the backs
of my hands as a promise
meeting its intention Inside the furniture
is growing through the rug

Huge with froth wakes the tugs
and others with tires
and disagreeing engines
vaguely discernible dark shapes move
ponderous as dread on water and earth
massive unknowable dim loads
Tiny lights within like cities on the move
It may be exactly as some feared
a penitent traffic of black acts
is being rearranged at night
over and over forever
day's hidden guilts working a penance
the questionable commerce of mere hearts
and in each one a window
a small required figure at a wheel

from *STARS ON A WIRE* (1989)

AH MAHOGANY

We know so little directly.
Trees must break into rooms
before we know them,
into parquetry and floor.
Then we say, Ah, Mahogany,
and learn the knots and grains
of skin covering our walls,
some finishes, the deep bright roots
in our eyes.

Memory is so breakable
we store it in things.
Objects become us like clothes
take on our shapes.
We choose them to be us;
we are revealed in the furniture.
Perhaps they drain us kindly
like photography. We touch them;
they take on our shine.

On my bookshelf with lean-to legs
there is some of me in your photo;
there is a tea ball in sterling.
We are coming apart together,
delicate and unexpected.
Room after room is full of us;
each book a part of our brains,

enamels, chocolate spoons,
shells and loose bones.

We can be put together again
a little, part by part.
When we are gone we will
no be quite gone.
To someone among our objects,
we will be more there.
Perhaps we gathered them
just for the purpose,
otherwise there would be only
dry parchment, tarnished negative,
veneers.

DARK LIKE BEING

When I am exhausted, when I seem to be
a man loaded with bones,
when we are in the deep of the day
and light cannot get down to us anymore,
as it cannot get down under the reef,
even thickened under air as under water,
and the birds have emptied their colors
over the horizon, the world left to us
is an old photo, deep ago, with no breathing.
We have useless eyes.

What happens at night is something
only another can tell you.
You brush me awake. —You mumbled,
your face flickered like inside your face
was on fire, there was something lost
on both sides of your pillow—
I remember now. It was dark like being
under water, like a photograph. It hurt to breathe.
The vet with a flashlight was showing me
the two small clouds in the dog's eyes.

STARS ON A WIRE

Before concertina was just a little shindig
keeping dancers within its music & a thornvive
slinky hemmed the bulldozing pigs and barnyard,
before these were come together in warfare
was the idea of barbed wire already in the dark
far-spread connect-the-dots of the sky.

Think of it, stars on a wire,

a chaos contained in the outlines of animals,
the path the moon-line passed through
made from the almost nothing of night;
the edge of a hunger & his bear whirled round
forever, strung to their battle, and on paper
courses plotted to shining islands of vellum
Indies: planets and ideas with little starbursts
of directed intentions, the sky and the mind
tied together.

Ideas with pictures pass through walls
like a window through the rocks of Lascaux,
layered glassy canvasses of skinglue & gesso.
open, even the mitered hardwoods of Duccio
made space on which a wizened child and a Mary
grew substantial with eggwhite and gold.

And there is the whiskered nose of the mole
in its tunnels, another picture starred with vibrissae,
the fence where farmers hang up their gloveskins,
prisoners attempting escape snagged on stars,
the killing lines of the tracers puncturing night.

The Renaissance discovered a progress
of bright spots shot through with perspective,
all their tall colonnades diminished together,
architecture strung itself up on new stars,
wired to the past like a telegraph
and we discovered it again and again
because we think along the same lines,
ideas flare up and may again, new-faced,
a smolder, a star, the plus, the asterisk, X,
where one line saws on another and multiplies.

NOTHING BUT SCAPULAE

At what point is the mind connected
to the body   well
just above the neck I think
where Aristotle's hot vapors of the heart
meet the chilly brain and clog
the eyes and nose with congestive fevers
—infection like a weather
and where are we connected to the angels   well
that is another matter

What arrogance that any glory we suppose
feathered with light
might have come from their heavens
to interbreed with us above all others
self-destructive worms
what evidence for this boast
—nothing but scapulae
bony shrunken useless for flying

But if I   working shoulders
like bird wings life off from you
or you lighter coming from clouds,
seem to hover above me
I feel a slight growth as if
something was blooming as if
I must lift up from the pillow
to accommodate wings

LOCAL INFLUENCE

Some gravity yes
but I would say fishes assist
in driving the rivers
As a stir imparts swirls
for which the spoon is responsible
likewise Mullet and Bluefish turn
the recurved gyres of the Gulf

Things *are* what they seem
Celery *is* constructed of lake ice & floss
What headlights sweep across dark rooms
are ghosts for a moment and out there
the occasional thin shadow of Earth
flickers over Andromeda and who knows
what is made of it

Influence works best at close range
People daily respond to the sign of the Discount
hoarding and selling under the influence
of the Handgun   the Oil Spill constellation
Those controlled like stars by the Wood's Night Voices
are parading in hospitals and on the roof
the rooster and the copper whale turn searching
like scouts   The stars camped in the night
are just fires of someone else's far argument

VECTORS OF CHANGE

The heron on the dock at high tide stares
over the edge at conventions of minnows
it cannot reach and entertains an idea
of the endless delicious populations
of the sea beyond shallows, and the strain
of longing for fathoms and dinner,
the singular pleasures imagined
of what could be the world's longest swallow,
that focused thought is recorded in notepads
unknown to the heron who is changing
the future by wishing and far off the unborn
of the unborn, in the endless unmentionable
heron suppositions of futurity
tiny eventual femurs stretch out, invisible
transparent bones of the neck lengthen

Acknowledgments

A New and Selected is a special kind of vantage, looking back over poems and publications of years of writing to see what's held up, what's holding up. It is also a recognition that such a look was warranted, and for that I am indebted to editor Jonathan Fink for having that opinion and offering that opportunity, and for the guidance and enthusiasm that made the process such a pleasure.

My very deep appreciation is due Stephanie Burt, whose continuous attention to my work over the years has been exceptional and generous. To have Stephanie write the introduction to this New and Selected is yet another charmed instance of that generosity, and I am very grateful for all of it.

A special thanks to the editors and publishers of the books and chapbooks that make up this volume: University of Massachusetts Press, Defined Providence Press, Bateau Press, McSweeney's, Salmon Poetry, 42 Miles Press, Tupelo Press, Right Hand Pointing, At Length, and the University of Alabama's Institute for the Book Arts.

I also wish to acknowledge the magazines in which some of the poems in the NEW section first appeared, some in slightly different versions: *Alligator Juniper; Concīs; The Gettysburg Review; The Nation; The Literary Review; Puerto del Sol; Mississippi Review; Redactions; Subtropics; Verdad; Zyzzyva*.

My sincere thanks also goes to a few of the other people over the years that recognized and promoted my work in various ways: Paul Sweeney, Dale Wisely, Jesse Nathan, Dominic Luxford, Mark Drew, Jeff Mock, Jessie Lendennie, David Dodd Lee, Sandra Williams, Kevin Prufer, Andrea Cohen, Cynthia Stephens, Liz Robinson, Elena Tomorowitz, Andrea Hollander, John Witte, Kristina Kearns, Simmons B. Buntin, and The Center for Writers at The University of Southern Mississippi. My apologies in advance for any omissions.

CREDITS

Calligraphy: Frances Dunham: *Fragile Acts; Stars on a Wire*
Cover Art: Jacob Magraw-Mickelson: *Fragile Acts*
Cover and Type Design: Michael Manoogian: *As Much As*
Book Design: Amy Borezo, Shelter Bookworks: *Omnivore*
Cover and Text Design: Bill Kuch: *Other Than They Seem*
Cover Photo: Allan Peterson: *Other Than They Seem*
Cover Art: Allan Peterson: *Any Given Moment; This Luminous*
Front Cover Design: Olivia Ashcraft: *This Luminous*

Special appreciation to Prof. Joseph Herring and student Olivia Ashcraft of the Department of Art at the University of West Florida for their collaborative efforts in creation of the front cover.

My sincere thanks to those magazines and journals where the poems first appeared, sometimes in somewhat different forms:

ACM Another Chicago Magazine, Famous Canaries; *Adirondack Review,* The Uses Of Nature; *Alligator Juniper,* Ex Libris, Wishing; *At Length,* The Natural World, Earth Science, Solving For X, Conservation Of Elegy, Losing Track; *Bayou,* Every Day; *Blackbird,* Whim Of The Minute; *The Believer,* Local News, What Was Saved; *Beloit Poetry Journal,* As If Galvanic; *Cascadia,* Category 2; *The Chattahoochee Review,* The Inevitable; *Concīs,* Optimism; *for poetry.com,* There I Go Again; *Full Circle Journal,* The Totality Of Facts; *Gettysburg Review,* Whether Neither, What Was Saved, Death About Love, Hitting The Hot Spots, Easy Believers, Reminders; *Girls With Insurance,* Task, What Was Saved; *Innisfree,* Frequent Flyer; *James River Review,* How; *Kennesaw Review,* Distraction; *The Literary Review,* Vignette, Sums, Translation; *Ladowich,* Atmosphere; *Mid-American Review,* I Know Ice; *Maryland Poetry Review,* Here At The Intersection; *Marlboro Review,* Grey Areas; *The Nation,* Koi; *Notre Dame Review,* Right Before Your Eyes, All This Instead; *The Panhandler,* Tropical Depression; *The Pedestal,* Making Sense; *Plains Poetry Journal,* Second Opinion; *Potomac,* Bad News Fast; *Puerto del Sol,* Handmade Experience; *Red Hills Reader,* Something Important; *Right Hand Pointing,* As Far As I Know, Nothing Predictable; *The Seventh Quarry,* Limitations; *Subtropics,* Outvoted; *Stickman Review,* No Gods Needed; *Story South,* Hurricane

In Halves, Long Distance; *Square Lake,* Knowledge First; *Talking River Review,* Wrong Number; *Tar Wolf,* Transplants; *Verdad, Lyric,* How It Works.

And a special thanks to McSweeney's: The Totality Of Facts; Hunger For Substances; More; *In the society of glass . . . ;* It was like a laser . . . ; It was the heron . . . ; Knowing What I Know Now; Grey Areas; Frequent Flyer; Local News; *There was an Era of Ashes . . . ;* We lived in these bodies . . . ; The body was not a book . . . ; Negotiating With Details; Long Distance; *There were echoes . . . ;* Let's say it took acres . . . ; Let's say the wet sky . . . ; Famous Canaries; Needless; Hitting The Hot Spots; Here At The Intersection.

Chronology

2016   *Other Than They Seem*

Tupelo Press, winner of the 2014 Snowbound Chapbook Prize

Judge, Ruth Ellen Kocher

2014   *Precarious*

42 Miles Press, selected by The Chicago Tribune as one of the four best poetry books of the year.

Editor, David Dodd Lee

2012   *Fragile Acts*

McSweeney's, #2 in the McSweeney's Poetry Series

Finalist for The National Book Critics Circle and Oregon Book Awards.

Editors, Jesse Nathan, Dominic Luxford

2011   *As Much As*

Salmon Poetry Press, Cliffs of Moher, County Clare, Ireland

Editor, Jessie Lendennie

2010   from *None Other*

At Length Magazine, Section 1 of an unpublished manuscript

Editor, Jonathan Farmer

2009   *Omnivore*

Bateau Press, winner of the 3rd Annual Boom Chapbook Prize

Editor, James Grinwis

2006   *All The Lavish In Common*

University of Massachusetts Press, 2005 Juniper Prize

2005   *Any Given Moment*
        Right Hand Pointing, online chapbook, righthandpointing.net
        Editor, Dale Wisely

2002   *Anonymous Or*
        2001 Defined Providence Press Prize
        Editor, Gary Whitehead

1994   *Small Charities*
        University of West Florida
        Editor, Laurie O'Brian

1989   *Stars On A Wire*
        Parallel Editions, University of Alabama Institute for the Book
        Arts, Sharon Long, Jean Buescher (Bartlett), designer/printers;
        Advisors, Steve Miller, Paula Gourley
        Reissued 2008 online by Right Hand Pointing

ALLAN PETERSON is the author of five previous books: *Precarious* (42 Miles Press, 2014); *Fragile Acts* (McSweeney's Poetry Series, 2012), a finalist for both the 2013 National Book Critics Circle Award and Oregon Book Awards; *As Much As* (Salmon Poetry, 2011, Ireland); *All the Lavish in Common* (University of Massachusetts Press, 2006), winner of the 2005 Juniper Prize for Poetry; *Anonymous Or* (Defined Providence Press, 2002), and eight chapbooks, including *Other Than They Seem* (Tupelo Press, 2016), winner of the Snowbound Chapbook Award, and *Omnivore* (Bateau Press, 2009), winner of the BOOM Chapbook Prize.

He has received fellowships from the National Endowment for the Arts and the State of Florida and was the American invited to the 2010 Cuisle Limerick City International Poetry Festival, Ireland. Other recognitions include poetry panelist, Conference on World Affairs, University of Colorado, Boulder; Ted Kooser's American Life in Poetry Series (#159); American Poet Prize, Arts & Letters Poetry Prize; GSU Poetry Prize; Muriel Craft Bailey Poetry Prize; Words & Images Poetry Prize.

His work has appeared nationally and internationally in print and online for many years and has been anthologized in *American Poetry at the End of the Millennium* and *Literature of the American Apocalypse* by *Green Mountains Review*, 2000 and 2005; *The Southern Poetry Anthology*, Texas A&M University Press; *The Emily Dickinson Award Anthology 2000*, and elsewhere. Essays on his work are included in Stephen Burt's *Close Calls with Nonsense: Reading New Poetry* (Graywolf Press, 2009) and *The Poem Is You: 60 Contemporary American Poems and How to Read Them* (Belknap Press, 2016).

As visual artist, he has exhibited widely and taught for seven years at the State University of New York, Geneseo, after which he became Art Department chair and director of the Anna Lamar Switzer Center for Visual Arts at Pensacola State College in Florida. He retired in 2005.

www.allanpeterson.net

CPSIA information can be obtained
at www.ICGtesting.com
Printed in the USA
FSHW011934010719
59631FS